AF323705

Praise for *Before You Love Again*

Janet St. Marie is a seeker. Determined to learn the secrets to being the master of her own destiny and happiness, Janet has accumulated a wealth of knowledge in the field of self-development and personal growth, applying and testing it in her own personal laboratory of self-love as she went along. The result is that now she has compiled the best of what she has learned and used to give us a heartfelt book filled with wisdom as well as whimsy.

While the subject of love is of course huge, Janet sets the stage by deftly taking the reader through an allegorical visualization of the process of going from battered and bruised by love lost, to being fully in charge of our own experience of love.

She then teaches us, step-by-step, several well-established techniques for emotional self-management, while gently guiding us in understanding the physiological, neurological and intellectual components of what drives our emotional experience.

I am delighted to have known Janet the past 10 years. She sometimes takes on the role of cheerleader, reminding me of my worth if I lapse into forgetfulness. And now she is the cheerleader for her readers, encouraging them on their journey of discovering their own brilliance and worthiness. And what a rewarding journey it is!

~ Meryl Hershey Beck, Author of
*Stop Eating Your Heart Out: The 21-Day Program
to Free Yourself from Emotional Eating*

Before You Love Again

From Relationship Misery...to Love Mastery!

Janet St. Marie

Before You Love Again
Copyright ©2014 by Janet St. Marie. All Rights Reserved.

The author of this book does not dispense medical advice or prescribe the use of any technique as a form of treatment for physical, emotional, or medical problems without the advice of a physician, either directly or indirectly. The intent of the author is only to offer information of a general nature to help you in your quest for well-being. In the event you use any of the information in this book for yourself, which is your constitutional right, the author and publisher assume no responsibility for your actions.

For information about this title or to order other books and/or electronic media, contact the publisher:
Janet St. Marie
Janet@InstituteOfSacredIntent.com

Author's Styling and Photo by EchoStarmaker.com

ISBN: 978-1-61961-912-8
Printed in the United States of America

Dedication

I dedicate this book to my father, Claude,
who was the most humble, gentle embodiment
of love I have met in my life's journey

AND

To my children — Jimmy, Erin, Megan, Kevin,
Kerry, Britta, and John — my greatest teachers.

Table of Contents

PART II
ENERGETICALLY SPEAKING   45

Acknowledgements

MANY MILLION THANKS go to my spiritual compadres — Teressa Fenison, Robin Trainor Masci, Rev. Donald Graves, Meryl Hershey Beck and Carol Cummings — who continually inspire me.

And to Mike Willams whose creative mind tweaked crucial aspects of this book.

And to my Lioncrest editors, Emil Prelic and Saundra Halgrimson, the talented possessors of great patience and wisdom.

A special thanks goes to Lynn Crozier who stood with me and lovingly supported me in confronting my false identities as I signed on the dotted line.

Without these people I can guarantee that *Before You Love Again* would still be hung up in Pure Potential somewhere.

Introduction

Love has no other desire but to fulfill itself.
But if you love and must needs have desires,
let these be your desires:
To melt and be like a running brook
that sings its melody to the night.
To know the pain of too much tenderness.
To be wounded by your own understanding of love;
And to bleed willingly and joyfully.
To wake at dawn with a winged heart
And give thanks for another day of loving;
To rest at the noon hour and
meditate love's ecstasy;
To return home at eventide with gratitude;
And then to sleep with a prayer for the
beloved in your heart
and a song of praise upon your lips.
~Kahlil Gibran

WHO AMONG US hasn't been hurt in our quest for love? No one.

It's not just the "unlucky," or those too afraid to let love in. In this physical world of limitation and restriction we all inhabit––the beautifully expansive nature of love takes a hit in ways we all must endure.

As a Certified Energy Coach, as well as a Certified "Calling In The One" Coach, I've shared with my clients the truth that the innate power each of us holds is our ability to create a life of absolute love, *no matter what.* **We ARE the Love we are seeking from someone else.**

We already **are** love. But we don't believe it. We cover it up in ourselves, or deny it, or try to destroy it. And we will fight to the death to disown it.

Until we know better, we reject…deflect…or neglect… love.

How fierce are the opposing forces within us! Our fear of intimacy, one of the deepest core level fears we have, is perhaps the greatest battleground. We're afraid of intimacy with another — it might mean rejection. But even worse, we fear intimacy with ourselves because we know first hand how capable we are of rejecting our very own "Self".

There is a wonderful Native American story that hits this nail squarely on the head. Grandfather, a wonderful sage, was sitting and speaking to his grandchildren one day. He said, "Grandchildren, I have a battle going on within me, like two wolves fighting each other. One wolf is of love. And the other wolf is of anger. Both wolves try to dominate my spirit and sometimes it's hard to live with them."

The grandchildren were enthralled and aghast as they looked at him wide-eyed. And then one of them anxiously asked him, "Grandfather, which wolf wins?"

And he replied, simply, "The one that I feed."

We all have a deep desire to be loved, to be accepted for who we *are*; not for what we do. We seek closeness, physically and emotionally. We seek intimacy or "Into Me See." If just one other person, in this sea of seven-plus billion, gets us…really gets us…we feel at the core of our being that we might be worthy enough to be alive. It makes us feel okay in the world, and that we have value in this thing called Life.

Why, then, are we so terrified of intimacy?

Because at a core level we believe that we need to deserve love and that we fall far short of being worthy. We're drawn towards intimate sexual connection with another individual and yet deeply afraid of seeking it because we know that human beings are wonderfully changeable creatures——they can be here one day, gone the next. We run from intimacy because being fully known ("warts and all") and then possibly being rejected or abandoned would catapult us into the cauldron of soul searing agony.

More deeply embodied within us, beneath our battles with fear and isolation and self-protection, is the ultimate question that we all hunger to resolve: How do we truly exist in a space of freedom?

Freedom in our very souls.

Freedom not contingent on what others think or say or do.

Freedom in our heart-of-hearts, the deepest level of our being, from which our every action would spring forth to create safety, and even peace, in our existence.

The answer…is Love. I'm not talking about "airy-fairy" or Beatle's songs or Tinker Bell dust kind of stuff. This is the **real thing**. We must follow the call of an inner wisdom that resides in the deepest part of us in order to rise above the ego's dictates. This is not the wisdom of our thoughts but the wisdom of our *knowing*. It emerges from the place of who we "are" — the true us, free of the ego's yammering. This place is the deep, eternal space we sense in the core of our body, nestled inside the protection of our ribs — our immortalized heart.

The human heart (spiritual or physical — the energies are inextricably united) has its own intelligence and electromagnetic field. And the supreme harmonic wave rhythm of the heart is love. In all its forms — especially in its most intimate form — love affords us the way into superb health and even more importantly the way out of the ego's highly prized, but crushingly painful, world of Aloneness. For some people the proof of, and the experience of, the harmonic supremacy of love is a huge chasm to cross, a huge leap to take!

It doesn't have to be.

Part I of this book — "Allegorically Speaking" — is a fable of sorts. It begins with a simple story of a character named Tender Heart, who learns how and why the Path of Love has been so difficult for her. She learns to free herself from past heartache and enter a very different reality.

If you're not interested in fables or allegories, and want to "cut to the chase" of the "How To" information, just skip

Part I. However, please know that you may find this story worth reading as it will prepare you in a profound way for the learning that follows.

Part II of the book — "Energetically Speaking" — reveals and explores the energetic aspects of human relationships and how they lead *us* into *our* relationship predicaments.

More importantly, this book gives you some simple, proven tools created by therapists and other experts in the field of Energy Psychology, which you will have from this day forward to use in creating a new reality that literally brings love into your life.

Come take a leap with me.

Into the world of true love.

Into the world of your Tender Heart, the hero of your story.

P A R T I

Allegorically Speaking

The Story of Your Tender Heart

THE LONG DARK ROAD

TENDER HEART stood there all alone, terrified, in the fatal darkness of the most desolate road she'd ever traveled. Not knowing which way to turn, she stood paralyzed. The deafening pounding inside her chest was the only palpable evidence of anything alive in the entire grizzly area. As she tried to figure out where she was, in this the blackest moment of her life, she realized she was hopelessly and forever lost.

But she knew she had to keep going. She had to choose which fork in the road to keep traveling down. Or just die right there. One gnarly trail looked as horrid as the other so it made no difference to her which one she would pick. Nothing had ever worked before…none of her choices had led to her long-anticipated destination.

How had she ever gotten to this God-forsaken place in her life? And how could she ever get out of here? She didn't even know what kind of journey she was on any more. All she'd ever known was step-by-step…every day…day after day. And it had gotten her nowhere but here in this dark and devastating place.

What Tender Heart did not know was that she had embarked upon on a road that is very difficult to navigate without the use of very specific tools to assist. As she discovered over the years this road was very twisted, agonizingly steep at times, annoyingly circuitous, and often hopelessly confusing. But what she hadn't discovered yet is that this road can lead to unspeakable, indescribable amazement and fulfillment — if she stays the course. It's called the Path of Love. And it can be a stern teacher — until we learn to master it. *This* Tender Heart would do. She would learn that the mastery of love is the alignment with it.

You see, Tender Heart had been struggling for years on this Path of Love. Ever since childhood, she'd felt the sting of being ignored and her little child brain dealt with it the only way it knew — to be "invisible." That way it didn't hurt so much. Of course no one could notice her because SHE decided that they wouldn't. And so she remained behind her walls of protection up to this day of abject darkness.

All she wanted was love. And in her search for it all these years on this rocky Path of Love, she'd often felt bloodied from the tiny jagged rocks that tore at her feet.

While she trod cautiously along in fear of the rocks, she collided headlong into treacherous boulders, the size of crouching tigers, bruising her tender body.

But those towers. Oh, those dreaded towers.

These huge rocky spires that blocked her path at regular intervals seemed familiar, as though they held some special meaning. Some of the pinnacles were lopsided as though tilted from unbalanced weight. Others had impenetrable facades gradually eroding into putty. Still more had wide cracks between wedges that clung tightly to each other stretching as one edifice into the sky. Although she didn't yet know it, each was a tower of boulder piled upon boulder telling her story. Enormous and powerful as they were, they looked as weathered and beaten as she felt; and to her they all were as threatening as anything had ever been in her life. They had a funny name: "Hoodoos." Each of them was a huge trauma for her and their massive, unrelenting presence stopped her in her tracks until she "invisibled" her way around them.

Her entire body was bruised, and her psyche was completely battered from bashing into insensitive and un-trustable people on the road. But beyond all that, her heart — the only thing that was keeping her going — was now beginning to die from the dejection she was consumed in.

Every now and again, as she trudged along with so many other angrily dying people, she'd see a bright and happy soul coming from the direction they were all going towards. She wondered about such beings, but always just kept going on, with the sad knowing that her trek would never end. Day after day she'd walk the walk of despair.

A MOMENT OF COURAGE

A T THIS PARTICULAR MOMENT, as Tender Heart stood paralyzed in total wretchedness, she noticed a glimmer of light flickering in the horrid darkness. As the glow inched its way towards her and grew in dimension and intensity, she recognized its essence as one of those bright and radiant beings walking towards her. Tender Heart, in spite of her desperation (but more likely because of it), set aside all her inhibitions and gathered enough courage to make eye contact. This gesture captured the glowing being's attention, who smiled at her and then stopped in front of her.

There was immense kindness in this stranger's eyes and Tender Heart felt comforted, yet also strangely intimidated. She had an inkling that in the next moments, her life could completely change. She quickly formulated in her mind what she was about to say to the stranger and gathered the courage to speak. Somehow, and with great determination, Tender Heart found her voice and squeaked out the wobbly words:

I am so sorry to bother you. Can I please talk to you for a moment?

The stranger replied.
OF COURSE. WHAT CAN I DO FOR YOU?

There was a bit of a pause as Tender Heart was still summoning courage. So the stranger took the opportunity to introduce herself.

MY NAME IS BELLA DIVINA.
AND I'M VERY PLEASED TO MEET YOU,............

Oh.
Ohhh.
I'm Tender Heart. And I'm really glad to meet
you.

It was then that the being noticed the hopeless
fatigue that circled Tender Heart's eyes.

YOU LOOK MIGHTY TIRED. AND A LITTLE LOST.
ACTUALLY YOU'RE PRETTY MUCH ON SCHEDULE,
TENDER HEART. MOST PEOPLE FEEL LIKE GIVING
UP BY THIS JUNCTURE IN THE ROAD BECAUSE THEY
CAN'T SEE AHEAD TO VIEW WHAT THEY'RE ABOUT
TO GET INTO. AND THEY'RE REALLY TIRED OF
WHAT THEY'VE ALREADY BEEN THROUGH.
WHAT CAN I HELP YOU WITH? DO YOU NEED
DIRECTIONS?

(Oh, boy. Do I.) Tender Heart thought to herself.
(In all kinds of ways…)

I was just wondering. You look so happy. Where
did you come from and how can I get there?
I'm so sick of all this pushing and shoving and
falling and bleeding and heartache. I'm so, so
tired of all the jerks who told me they loved me
and then left. I cannot go through one more

betrayal or one more breakup, or any more rejection. I'm just so done!

Bella Divina looked at her with great compassion in her eyes and spoke from a place of deep understanding.

Yes. I'm sure. The pain from all of that is excruciating.
I know those days well.

Really??

Oh, my heavens, yes. And i also now know that there is a way out of all of it.
I can show you, if you'd like.

Oh, my gosh yes! Yes, yes, yes! Can we start now?

Bella thought a moment and then answered.

It's a process, Tender Heart.
And it's a little rough in the beginning.
But if you do what i share with you, you'll reach the end of this road.

A process? What kind of process? Can it be rougher than what I've gone through already? I don't think so.

It's just a different kind of rough. And worth every bit of the ride. Would you like to try it? You can quit at any time, if you'd like, and simply stay on the road.

A WILLINGNESS TO TRY

Tender Heart was intrigued and hugely motivated to leave the treacherous path as quickly as was humanly possible. So she vigorously nodded her head in affirmation followed by a thank you to Bella for being willing to help her.

Let's do this.

Since *NOW* is always the perfect time, they began walking the journey learning about each other's histories and the reasons they were on the path. Tender Heart continued to tear the skin of her feet and legs on those God-awful rocks and boulders while Bella Divina seemed to glide right over them without a notice. Before long, Bella stopped their forward motion and instructed Tender Heart:

All right, my dear. This is where you begin.

Bella turned around, and Tender Heart automatically turned with her, to assess the terrain they'd just traveled.

First, you need to go back on the road and find those jagged rocks that you've stumbled over. And here's why: those rocks that tripped you up are the *negative thoughts* you formed from the rejections

AND TRAUMAS AND UNHAPPY ENCOUNTERS YOU
EXPERIENCED IN YOUR LIFE.

YOU NEED TO PICK THEM UP, ALL OF THEM THAT
YOU RECOGNIZE, AND BRING THEM HERE.
WE'LL FIND A PLACE THAT IS QUIET AND OUT OF
THE WAY, OFF THE ROAD RIGHT HERE, WHERE
YOU CAN PUT THEM.

**Rejections? Traumas? Negative encounters
and thoughts?
I don't understand. What does that all mean?
And who cares?
That was all *then,* and we're here now. Why do
I have to bother with them? Besides, it's going
to take such a long time.
How will I find all of them?**

Bella Divina smiled at this, the first complaint,
because she knew that after Tender Heart got
used to the process she would become enchanted
with it. Or at least with the relief and strength
she received from it.

JUST GO BACK AND SEARCH. DO THE BEST YOU
CAN.

**Oh, man! There'll be so many. What do I do
with all of them?**

You'll place them in a pile right here. I'll keep watch, and wait for you.

It was a big job, but at last Tender Heart picked out and pried up all the jagged gravel she could find that she had stumbled over. She placed the stones in a pile bigger than she would have liked anyone to see. But it was her very own piece-by-piece pile so she embraced it. Figuratively speaking, that is.

When she was finally done, she sat down to take a little break, and after some time of stillness she asked:

What now, Bella?

Bella Divina picked up a stone and began rubbing it with a cloth that she always kept in her pocket. As she polished the spiny shard, Bella divulged the wisdom behind her actions.

You will clean each rock to make certain that it can never hurt you again. By so doing you will smooth the jagged edges and clear away the pain they've caused you. This is an important process to learn, because from this moment on you will forever be able to use it in times of need.

She handed the neophyte the cloth and said:

NOW TAKE EACH STONE AND CLEAN IT, JUST LIKE I SHOWED YOU.

So, over the next several days, Tender Heart cleaned and cleaned. She thought it was sort of like the "wax on wax off" young Daniel had to do in the movie "The Karate Kid." His assignment to wax the car over and over again seemed like the most obnoxious waste of time to him. But through the wise counsel of Mr. Miyagi, his mentor and karate teacher, Daniel learned that it was the process that was valuable, not the layers of wax. It was the patience, the calmness, and the learned endurance from the repetitive motions that were the lesson. It was never about a shiny car. It was about stamina and transformation.

Tender Heart's cleaning process (her "wax on, wax off") was, in our reality, a simple yet powerful Energy Technique called EFT, which you will learn later in the book, and which can lead to your transformation. Once learned, it is yours forever.

Tender Heart noticed that over less time than anyone would have thought, the rocks were getting shinier and shinier. Some were more resistant and took more effort than others to clean. As she worked feelings would well up in her, seemingly out of nowhere. There were times when Tender Heart became so angry she wanted to throw a certain stone or demolish the entire pile. Sometimes she cried softly as she polished yet another kind of pebble. A few times she sobbed and sobbed as though her heart were going to shatter into one final heartbreak. There were times that she felt very little emotion, but knew the item in front of her needed cleaning and just kept rubbing.

So many times she wanted to give up. But she stuck with it and found that with each and every fully cleaned and polished stone she always felt great relief.

As she got into the process she observed that the work was beginning to go much more quickly. Sometimes when she polished one stone, ten more she hadn't even touched yet instantly shimmered along with it. It seemed like a magical process. And she, herself, began to lighten up as well. She was actually becoming happier and more animated and even began to whistle while she scrubbed.

At last, the final bunch of formerly gunky trouble-makers glistened. What had been grossly jagged, grimy things were transformed into a stockpile of transparent, smooth, soft, gem-like pebbles that she could actually see through.

Tender Heart was tired but not the awful, hopeless tired she had known before. It was an invigorated tired — something she'd not felt in a very long time. And she liked it. A lot.

GREAT JOB, MY DEAR FRIEND! YOU WERE VERY THOROUGH.

Bella Divina handed her a nice big glass of cool, refreshingly pure water, which she accepted eagerly.

THERE'S ONE MORE THING TO DO IN THIS PHASE, TENDER HEART.

The student looked over the rim of her glass at Bella with eyebrows raised questioningly as she kept drinking.

A CHALLENGE OF MIGHTY PROPORTIONS

Bella Divina continued:

NOW YOU NEED TO GO BACK AND COLLECT THE
BOULDERS THAT TORE AT YOUR LEGS AND THAT
BLOODIED YOU SO BADLY ON THE ROAD.
THESE BOULDERS ARE THE LARGER, HARSHER
BELIEFS YOU FORMED IN YOUR LIFE THAT MADE
YOUR FORWARD PROGRESS SO DIFFICULT.

Tender Heart nearly choked on the glug of water
she'd been relishing.

**I have to go back? Those crappy boulders now?
Harsher beliefs? Are you kidding me? Do you
know how painful they are? Do you have any
idea how much those things hurt? I never want
to go near them again.**

But guess what. Tender Heart did it, blind faith
leading the way. It took quite a bit of time, but she
dug and shoved and shimmied and rolled each
tiger size boulder over to the side of the road near
her pile. She cleaned these structures using another
procedure, which Bella taught her.

When she was done, and heaved all the extra weight
and bulk of them on to her now small mountain,
she felt quite satisfied at her accomplishment.

In our reality, this new procedure is another Energy Technique you will learn in this book, called RITT, which also is yours forever once you learn it.

Bella Divina beckoned her to sit down and rest at the base of the mound. And after a little time of silence, the bright being spoke.

THESE ROCKS IN YOUR PILE, TENDER HEART, ARE THE *NEGATIVE THOUGHTS* YOU'VE HARBORED, ALL ALONG YOUR WAY, AGAINST YOUR MOTHER... FATHER...LIFE... GOD...SIBLINGS...TEACHERS... AUTHORITY FIGURES...FRIENDS...CO-WORKERS... BOSSES...NEIGHBORS...LOVERS...CHILDREN... STRANGERS...FOREIGNERS...PEOPLE WHO SCARED YOU BECAUSE THEY WERE DIFFERENT...AND ANY ONE ELSE YOU CAN THINK OF.

THEY CAUSED YOU TO STUMBLE AND THEY MADE YOUR TRAVELS DIFFICULT. THEY IMPEDED YOUR PROGRESS EVERY DAY OF YOUR LIFE, BUT YOU DIDN'T EVEN KNOW WHAT THEY WERE WHEN YOU TRIPPED OVER THEM. AND YOU CERTAINLY DIDN'T KNOW THAT YOU HAD PLACED THEM THERE BEFORE YOU EVEN STEPPED ON TO THE PATH OF LOVE.

Balk!!!...

Tender Heart stiffened, bristling at the idea that she was causing her own suffering...that simply wasn't true! She couldn't possibly have created this horrible, painful experience in her own life. Or DID she??

YES, YOU DID. EVERY TIME YOU CHOSE TO JUDGE AND CRITICIZE AND BE UNGRATEFUL YOU PLACED A STONE THAT WOULD HURT YOU ON YOUR PATH.

AND THEN YOU ADDED THOSE LARGE BOULDERS TO BUMP INTO. THEY ARE THE HARDENED BELIEFS YOU FORMED ABOUT MEN...WOMEN...RELATION-SHIPS...AND LIFE IN GENERAL. THESE *NEGATIVE CORE BELIEFS* ARE BARRIERS IN NEARLY EVERY MOMENT OF YOUR LIFE.

BECAUSE OF PAST HURTS YOU BELIEVED CERTAIN NEGATIVE THINGS ABOUT SPECIFIC PEOPLE IN YOUR LIFE. THEN YOU EXPANDED THOSE BELEIFS TO INCLUDE ALL OTHER PEOPLE WHO RESEMBLE THEM IN SOME WAY.

BUT THE BELIEFS THAT HARM YOU THE MOST, AND STOP YOU POINT-BLANK ON THE ROAD TO LOVE, ARE YOUR *CORE FALSE IDENTITIES.* THESE ARE BELIEFS YOU MADE UP ABOUT WHO *YOU* ARE, BASED ON THOSE SAME NEGATIVE ENCOUNTERS YOU'VE HAD. THESE FALSE IDENTITIES WILL CAN-CEL, *EVERY TIME,* THE POSSIBILITY OF BRINGING IN THE DEEP AND ABIDING LOVE THAT YOU REALLY WANT IN YOUR LIFE. THESE ARE THE HOODOOS;

THEY STOP YOUR FORWARD MOVEMENT, AND YOU CANNOT "INVISIBLE" YOUR WAY AROUND THEM BECAUSE, MY DEAR BEAUTIFUL TENDER HEART:

THESE IDENTITIES RESIDE WITHIN YOU.

THAT'S HOW POWERFUL YOU ARE.
YOU FORMED THEM BEFORE YOU WERE EVEN AWARE OF THEM.
AND THEY HAVE BEEN WAITING FOR YOU TO FINALLY SEE THE LANDSCAPE YOU'VE CREATED.

YOU ARE YOUR OWN BIGGEST STOPPER.

Stunned. That's what Tender Heart was. **Stunned.**

READY TO CHANGE

Happily, Tender Heart's understanding was opened enough by the collecting and the cleaning she had done that she was able to hear Bella's words.

She stammered out the question:

But how? How did I become my own biggest stopper?

Bella explained to Tender Heart ***how*** she had created her "false identities." And she taught her ***how to clean*** them by giving words to those insidious beliefs with a very special, very thorough tool.

*In our reality, the "**how**" that Bella taught her is the "Cycle of Re-Creation", which you will learn and become skilled in tracing for yourself. And the "**how to clean**" is the tool called "I Am Statements," from which you will glean profound insight. Both are incredible exercises of precision that gently get to the deepest core of suffering.*

Tender Heart knew, without being told, what she needed to do next. So she went back to the few enormous stoppers she'd created, and over the next few days, she cleaned the 'negative' off, just the way Bella had taught her. Once done, she realized they had actually diminished in size and weight. And to her delight, she was able to drag them over to her pile.

Tender Heart sat by the base of the now mini-mountain. As her gaze settled on the clear, polished rocks and boulders and pillars that once had been so painfully damaging, she realized that all the work she did cleaning them had actually turned them into something different. These were her old thoughts and beliefs, transformed. Where before they had been ugly, and painful to step on and bang into, now they were translucent enough that she could see through each and every one. They became, for her, lovely prisms reflecting the understanding she'd gained from clearing them. And now they no longer held the harsh meanings that they had before. She could appreciate them as the structures that they were. Structures into which she had the power to place any meaning she chose. Tender Heart realized that she didn't want to even bother putting meanings into them. They simply didn't matter to her anymore.

As she was reflecting about all this, Bella Divina asked her:

IS THERE ANYTHING MORE THAT YOU NEED TO DO WITH YOUR THOUGHTS AND OLD BELIEFS AND IDENTITIES?

I don't think so.

DO YOU FEEL COMPLETE?

LIKE YOU COULD LEAVE THEM BEHIND AND MOVE ON?

Oh, Yes.

ARE YOU READY THEN?

Yes. Yes I am.

WELL THERE IS ONE LAST THING YOU MUST DO.

In the rather pregnant pause, Tender Heart waited…and waited…until she felt an urgent need to fill the silence with the obvious question. And Bella waited…and waited… for just the right moment to lay it on Tender Heart. She knew the reaction that was going to erupt.

What do I have to do now, Bella?

WELL, MY SWEET, YOU MUST DESTROY THIS PILE.

What??!!

Tender Heart all but jumped up and down and stamped her feet. She'd worked so hard! Not only was she in disbelief at such a bright and joyous being talking of destruction — the very idea! More than that, she'd grown rather attached to the hard work she'd done… and the shiny trophies to prove it.

YOU MUST BLOW IT ALL UP. BE DONE WITH IT.

Tender Heart sharply drew in her breath. How violent!

But all of a sudden it seemed appropriate. Those thoughts and beliefs had been so violent for her. And she didn't want them or need them anymore.

YOU DON'T WANT TO TRAVEL A PATH LIKE THIS ANY MORE. IS THAT CORRECT?

Correct. Never again!

YOU'RE READY FOR SOMETHING NEW. IS THAT CORRECT?

Bella, all my life this kind of path is all I knew. I truly don't want to go this way anymore. I just don't know a new way. But I know I don't want this.

GOOD ENOUGH. I WILL GIVE YOU THE MATERIALS TO INCINERATE THIS PILE.

While Bella Divina was busy "materializing" the materials, Tender Heart was busy messing up her mind.

(I said I was finished. Am I really? If I let go of these rocks and boulders and hoodoos, then what?
They don't have the awful meanings they once had, so maybe I can just keep them around as remembrances.
How would I haul them around from now on?
Do I even want to haul them around?
But I don't really need them.
I don't even want them.
If I truly let go of all the meanings I've made in my life, then who will I be without them?
I don't know.)

{Gulp}

(I feel like I'm done with them, but what if I need some for the rest of my journey? They got me this far.
Right. Look where they got you. Look at how awful your trip this far has been.
You didn't do all the work you just did for nothing.)

When Tender Heart finished with the back-and-forth of her thoughts she saw Bella standing peacefully, waiting patiently for her to proceed.

Shall we?

Yup. Let's do it before I change my mind.

Okay, sweetie.

You must, with all your heart and all your desire, give words to what it is that you want from this point on.

Tender Heart thought a while about the words she would say. But she knew, as she had known all along, what her heart's desire had always been. She'd never spoken the words out loud much less with all her heart. She felt awkward and silly. Oops. Two more stones to throw in the pile. So she cleared them and threw them in. After a little while she bravely spoke up:

Okay. I'm ready. Let's do this.

Now, with all your heart and all your mind and all your soul, say your words. And *feel* them.
This is the most important part.
Feel, with all that's in you, what you desire from the center of your heart.

A small tear slid out of the corner of Tender Heart's eye and she began to sob ever so gently — just a whisper of a sob that was beginning to usher out her words.

And Bella Divina knew this to be the sign.

Bella gave her the materials and without much ado Tender Heart, tears in eyes, jammed them fiercely and completely into the center of the pile and lit the flame.

And the Words began. But they were more than just words. They were living, viable, palpable realities. It was as though they were pulling the deepest recesses of her soul out into the air around her. She could feel the vibration of them as they passed through her body on the wings of her voice. Her deepest desire finally would be known as the words spoke themselves from the most intimate, sacred place inside her to the outer place of World.

Tender Heart looked to the heavens as if to give the Powers-That-Be the clear declaration: "This is it. This is the one thing that I want in all the world." Her words were firm in her mind, her tears were many, and her soul broke free from the tomb in which it had been lodged. And every ounce of energy she possessed shot into the universe.

She looked into the sky as though there were someone there to whom she was actually talking. She looked directly at the void and screamed out all that broke free from her.

I want to love and be loved !!

I want to love and be loved !!!!

I want to love and be loved !!!!!!

And with that, a mighty blast took her.

As she was reeling in the air, suspended in a new place, Tender Heart was not sure anyone had even heard her. All she knew was that her declaration had freed her. Whether or not she would ever find anyone to experience love with, her heart and soul were free. Surely a force of Love must exist, that this would happen to her.

It felt like some time had passed, but who knew? She was in a warp of nothingness, a vacuum of time, another dimension. It was there that she was held so lovingly and peacefully that she did not ever want to leave its weightless embrace. And in a way she never did. But she had to return to her journey. She had to go on.

A NEW WAY OF BEING

Tender Heart didn't wake up as if she had translocated from Kansas to Oz. What happened, though, was that a new road did, indeed, appear. It wasn't yellow brick, and it didn't lead to Emerald anything.

It took a while for her vision to clear. Or was it the smoke? Or was it a new ethereal dimension? Or was she in some play on a stage covered in vapors of dry ice? Or did her brain get shook into wafty? One thing for sure was that she was in a new and beautiful state of bewilderment.

So…now where was she going??

And who would be on this new road? What kind of people? How would they treat her? This was all a brand new adventure.

All Tender Heart remembered was saying, "**I want to love and be loved**" from the depths of her heart, then a flash, and then being different. She was in a new way of Being. The world had changed, or at least her inner world did. Nothing much changed in the outer world.

It was still the path, but a gentler path of soft, cushy mulch and pine needles. She noticed there was the tiniest hint of a few rocks. So tiny a hint, in fact, that she was not even sure that the rocks really existed, nestled among the needles and pieces of bark. And it didn't even much matter if they did exist because she knew how to transform them and make her journey more beautiful than it had ever been.

As she continued to travel, Tender Heart became aware of spectacular changes. Lush green grass sprouted up, a vibrant living carpet beneath villages of outrageously beautiful flowers that lined the edges of the path. And the unbelievably gorgeous colors spread out around her in every direction, towards an azure blue and puffy white horizon of cosmic art. Gently bent trees arched overhead to grace her travels with soft shade, and the "whoosh" of their wind-kissed leaves whispered a low humming sound in her ears. What an amazing vista was emerging before her, welcoming her into its wonderment.

This was still the Path of Love, yet this was a world of vision and expansiveness. No longer was she in the dark, dank prison of her previous world. In the first breath that she took here, she felt giddy with the weightlessness of freedom. It was in this experience of profound freedom that she realized how constricted and contracted her life before was. The air was so light and pure in this new world that she needed to get used to it. Tender Heart took a few deep and wonderful breaths, pulling in the pure and nourishing air.

As she began adjusting to this new existence she noticed a simple sign posted on the side of the cushiony road. It greeted her with a sweet yet puzzling message:

WELCOME HOME
TO THE FORCE AND FIELD OF LOVE

Her first thought was:
(Thank you. I think.)

Her second thought was:
(Home? What does that mean?)

Her third thought was:
(**Oh no. Where's Bella?**)

Here i am, darling. You didn't think i'd
leave you, did you?

**Actually, I didn't think anyone would survive
all that. Including me. That was pretty intense
back there.**

Yes. Wasn't it wonderful? Speaking your
deepest truth.

Mmm. It was intense.

**And now that I feel the way I do, I guess I'd
say it was wonderful.**
Who Knew?
**It feels so good here. I don't know how to
describe it, Bella. Mmmm.**

After a short while of meditative silence she said:

**This all feels like a huge hug. I feel like I belong
here… And I'm not alone. Like there's this big
entourage of invisible help here for me.**

That is the force of this field, it's a real
energy, Tender Heart. You may not see it
but you can feel it. And as you go along

THIS PATH YOU'LL LEARN TO RELAX INTO IT AND LIVE FROM IT.

THE WORLD OUTSIDE OF YOU WON'T BE ANY DIFFERENT; IT'LL ALWAYS HAVE ITS "ISSUES." BUT YOUR EXPERIENCE OF ITS CHALLENGES WILL BE RADICALLY DIFFERENT.

AS YOU CONNECT WITH THE FORCE OF THIS FIELD YOU WILL BE UNTOUCHED. THAT DOES NOT MEAN THAT HARSH THINGS WON'T HAPPEN, BUT WHEN YOU ARE ONE WITH THIS FORCE YOU WILL BE PROTECTED IN YOUR HEART OF HEARTS.

Whoa. You're getting' a little ahead of me here, Bella.
I just came from that world. I know what it's like.

I UNDERSTAND. I REALLY DO.
I KNOW IT WAS ROUGH FOR YOU.

Tender Heart could feel the empathy and compassion from Bella's heart, and just inhaled it as though she'd been without breath for lifetimes.

BEFORE WE GO ANY FARTHER DOWN THIS PATH OF DISCOVERY, THOUGH, THERE'S SOMETHING ELSE YOU MUST DO.

Groan…

Seriously?!
Seriously, Bella?!! Enough hasn't happened??

The being, in all her radiance, simply smiled. And then continued to explain:

You'll be traveling this new field using a new navigation system, with a compass that points to what truly *is*. You must accept what truly *is* or you will become lost again. It is the foundation of the direction you will take from here on.

This compass is also the reminder of the truth that resides *within* you and *as* you. You entered into the world *with* the truth, *as* truth. But you forgot, like all humans do. And your entire path, so far, has been about getting back to here — to this force and field.
To "home" — the force from which you came and the force that you are.

This compass represents the "*deeper truth of who you are.*" It always points to your personal north star and will guide you to your intended destiny.

YOU'LL KNOW WHEN YOU ARE FOLLOWING IT. THINGS WILL FEEL "JUST RIGHT" — LIKE MAMA BEAR'S THINGS IN THE TALE OF "GOLDILOCKS."

AND YOU'LL KNOW WHEN YOU'RE NOT. THERE WILL BE A SENSE OF "NOT RIGHT"NESS.

THE WAY MAY BE BUMPY, YOU MAY BE PULLED OFF COURSE AT TIMES, YOU MAY DRIFT FOR A WHILE. YOU MAY SIT IN A FOG OF CONFUSION AT JUNCTURES IN THE ROAD. BUT IF YOU TRUST YOUR INNER NAVIGATION — *THE DEEPER TRUTH OF WHO YOU ARE* — YOU WILL STAY THE COURSE AND END UP WHERE YOU'RE MEANT TO BE.

PEOPLE, PLACES AND EVENTS WILL COME ALONG TO CHALLENGE YOUR FUTURE DIRECTION IN LIFE. OF THIS YOU CAN BE SURE. BUT GREATER THAN ALL OF THOSE THINGS IS THE DEEPER TRUTH OF YOU.

While Tender Heart still had the memories of all the times in her life when she 'd created her beliefs and false identities, and how true they had seemed, now she no longer experienced the horrific pain of hating herself that came from believing them. She thought of the "I Am" statements she had learned about when she was taught to clean the hoodoos. How she'd shifted, and released her former beliefs of "I'm worthless and unloved and insignificant."

She remembered how she had transformed into knowing the deeper truth of who she was. That she was good and loveable and valuable.

Yes, she remembered feeling abandoned and rejected, alone and unloved back then. But now she realized that was all "outside" stuff. She at last knew she was not alone or unloved because love and completeness lived "within" her. She felt how fulfilling it was to appreciate this part of the path and she was able to relax into the absolute safety of this mysterious land.

And she began to remember more truths about herself:

She was not born to be alone.

The very fact that she exists means she has value.

*She was born **as** love, and she was born **to** love.*

She was born to be loved. And she is deeply loved by Love Itself!

She is a being of pure potentiality, and she is an integral part of the world.

She is a unique expression of the fullness and power of the force and field of Love, the Greater Reality.

What she does and how she behaves, has an impact on fellow beings.

As an ambassador of Love in the world, as an expression of its force, she stands as a testament to its power.

And with each breath, she drew what she now remembered about herself, into her herself. The knowledge of the deeper truth of who she really IS would reside in her the rest of her new way. The compass of this knowledge would keep her aligned with her True North, her destiny.

And she sought to make her new "knowings" even more clear, more succinct so they would be easy to remember. As she experimented, she came up with new "I Am" statements.

I AM PRECOUS

I AM VALUABLE

I AM COURAGEOUS

I AM GOOD

I AM LOVEABLE AND I AM LOVED

I Am Safe

I Am Wanted

I Belong

She refused to let her previous awful thoughts infiltrate and adulterate her newly discovered "knowings." When doubt sought a way in, she banished it before it could gain footing. When self-criticism and self-judgment sneaked in, she stomped on them fiercely.

Every now and then something would try to steal away her "knowings." But the certainty of who she truly was became so incorporated into her being that she was able to maintain her freedom from the self-loathing she'd lived in earlier on her path.

Jagged rocks of negative thoughts and judgments would intermittently appear before her. Some were rocks she threw down in the moment and some resurfaced from her previous life. Whatever few rocks lay along the path, she knew how to clean and transform them. There were no conflagrations or explosions when she did. Only popping sparks as the judgments and thoughts poofed into oblivion.

The boulders that appeared on the road were now simply empty bubbles which beckoned her to fill them in with new beliefs and perceptions that would enhance her future.

With each new encounter along the way, she was conscious and intentional about how she would continue to navigate the Path of Love. She no longer took things personally. And because of just this one simple choice she grew in loveliness and grace.

She no longer worried about bringing love into her life. She was becoming Love. Actually she always was Love. Just as we all are. But she, just as we, didn't believe it. She, just as we, covered it up and sabotaged it.

Her choices and actions were now emerging from her hard-won, well-deserved understanding of her true self. What a different way to live!

Tender Heart now understood she could make a difference in the world by the quality of the behaviors she was cultivating on the Path of Love. Her desire now was simply to **Be** Love in all her actions. However that "being-ness" would express itself in the world, she just wanted to **Be** Love. She hadn't learned the specific name of what this urge was, but she knew she had it. The force to which she had risen already was touching the lives of those who came into her field; and it was beginning to reach great distances. This is the power of the love she had discovered.

So Tender Heart kept going down this new path, the outward activities being the same as always. But inside her soul? What a magnificent change.

THE POWER IN BEING LOVE

ONE PARTICULAR DAY she was walking with Bella Divina past the beautiful lush grasses and flowers lining the path…just chatting away about nothing in particular.

They'd become like big sister and little sister. And Tender Heart so loved the relationship they'd been blessed with. What if she'd never asked for help that day? What if Bella hadn't come by at that moment of desperation? What if they hadn't locked eyes for that one split second? What if Tender Heart hadn't found the courage to speak up?

They came to a shaded spot where Bella chose to sit for a while. Tender Heart strolled a few paces away to pick some flowers nearby. Her mind was wandering as she reached for blooms of every color. She was delighting in the vaguely dancing thought forms in her mind, when in the distance, she could see a bright figure coming in waves towards her. As it weaved and bobbed in the vague shadows surrounding its form she felt a tiny stir within her heart. Something strange and wonderful about that figure was captivating to her. And yet she became afraid.

The space around her became electric.

Bella, who sensed this change, could see Tender Heart's light start to waver and she knew exactly what was happening. She smiled, and without Tender Heart having uttered a word Bella offered her a suggestion.

TENDER HEART, THERE IS ONE MORE THING YOU MUST DO.

You must create a ball of light.

Tender Heart's quietly frightened voice replied: **I don't know how to. I don't even know what you mean.**

It's really quite simple.
Here, let me guide you.
You begin by just seeing a ball of bright light in your imagination and keep building it.

Tender Heart closed her eyes and began first by imagining the brightness of the sun directly above her. From there she kept increasing the intensity of the light, as though stoking a fire. It became a pulsating ball of the whitest white she ever could fathom.

Now give it a size.

She made it the size of a, let's say……. a soccer ball.

Now make it look any way you want it to.
With facets like a diamond …. or with shooting rays coming from it… or glittery…. or spinning….
Any way you want it to look.

Tender Heart took her time and made it totally and exactly how she absolutely loved it to be.

Now hold the ball in your hands — outside of your body. Get a sense of its weight and density. And just keep holding it for a minute or so.

Tender Heart really felt that this ball of incredibly beautiful light that she'd created did indeed have some weight to it. Or maybe it was just her arms getting tired. When she thought that a minute or so had gone by, she let Bella know she was ready for the next instruction:

Okay.

Now bring the ball of light inside your body.

Tender Heart envisioned bringing the ball directly into her body and felt it pulsate within her, filling the entire space inside her rib cage. It was, after all, soccer ball size. She hugged herself real tight as if she were wrapping her body around the ball inside her torso. It felt so wonderful, this bright shimmery light.

All right. Now bring it outside of you again.

Hmm. This doesn't feel so nice, Bella. I kind of miss how wonderful it felt, now that it's outside of me. I feel a little darker inside. A little colder.

Bella smiled, and had her star pupil repeat this exercise a few more times.
Ball In — Ball Out….
Ball In — Ball Out…

So now can you identify the difference between when the ball is inside of you and when it's outside?

Oh, yes.

Which one feels better?

The ball being inside! It feels so energetic. And it feels comforting at the same time. How cool is that!? It fills me up and I feel warm, like everything's all right. It feels happy and fun. It feels even luscious. It feels like the most wonderful companion or friend. And I can take it anywhere.

I feel like a total package, complete and strong and even more "knowing" when the ball is inside of me.

Tender Heart,
This ball represents your *power*.
You created it. *You* gave it all its properties.
You placed it outside yourself, and *you* placed it inside.
You feel the difference when it's inside or out.

Remember what it feels like when your ball, your *power*, is inside of you. And remember how it feels when it's outside.

When you feel the ball outside of you, then it means you've just given your power away. To another person, to a thought, to a belief, to fear or anger, to whatever it is that you let that ball slip away to.

So just know that all you ever need to do is bring it back in.

Your goal is to live with your ball of light — your beautiful, energetic, warm, "everything's all right", luscious, knowing, strong *power* — inside of you every minute of every day.

Then Bella Divina looked in the direction of the approaching figure weaving in and through the shadows.

And now, dear Tender Heart, someone is finding his way to you. And you are being drawn to him.

I know. He's still all vague and fuzzy though. How will I know who he is, Bella?

It will be some time before you meet. You still have a good amount of time to prepare. And there are still things that must be done so that you will, indeed, recognize him.

Just stay on the path and keep evolving in the understanding of the deeper truth of who you are. I will teach you what you need to know. When we are finished you will recognize him. And he, you.

Go, Tender Heart.

Go to him, owning your beautiful power.

He, the one who resonates perfectly with you — your divine counterpart — is on his way.

PART II

Energetically Speaking

CHAPTER 1

We — As Pure Potential

"The source of all creation is pure consciousness...
pure potentiality seeking expression from the
unmanifest to the manifest. When we realize that our
true Self is one of pure potentiality, we align with the
power that manifests everything in the universe."
~Deepak Chopra, M.D.:
The Seven Spiritual Laws of Success

WE ALL START OUT as the proverbial "blank slate."
We arrive in this world *as* "pure potentiality," and as
such we enter this reality in a state of absolute openness. We
come from the world of all possibilities, and as its ambas-
sadors we are expressions of its fullness. In utero we are still
untouched by the physical world, so to speak, so there is
not yet any recognition of pain, and thus fear.

At the moment of birth we enter into the world of relationships and our potentiality starts to be contained and even programmed. We are handled by as yet unseen forces called doctors, nurses, and parents. We are wrapped, held, fed, and comforted — or not. The darkness and warmth we had floated in is replaced by bright lights and the coldness of temperature or non-connection.

And from there we grow up. Throughout our lives, at some indefinable level, everything that occurs in our lives has meaning. Everything "happens" exactly when and how it is supposed to happen at that moment. Everything. The good, the bad, and even the hideously ugly. As the philosopher Eckart Tolle tells us in his book, *A New Earth*: "Suffering has a noble purpose: the evolution of consciousness and the burning up of the ego."

The purpose of all that "happens" is to further evolution — both of our own personhood and all of humanity's. Actually all that happens **is** evolution. And in this physical reality we are the main players. You might think that's a stretch to imagine, but look at it this way: each and every one of us, with each and every passing moment in the remaining time available to the existence of earth, contributes to an ever-evolving reality. And our behaviors matter. In terms of our relationships, maybe they've have been messy, awful, or excruciatingly painful but it was all necessary to get us where we are right now, examining a different way.

We each have our own personalized, customized "lessons" to learn — and isn't *that* just something to wake up for each day? But, again, these are the stuff of our evolution. Some say these lessons come in with us when we are born.

Some claim that they come through the programming we received from authority figures and social environment. However our customized lessons present themselves, what we do *about* them, and with them, is the key to how successful and full our life will be.

It's all about the choices that we make. And these choices are based, in no small part, on the assumptions we form from deep-seated beliefs that we hold. And the places we get to test, confront, heal, and change these assumptions are point blank in the middle of our relationships.

In terms of our relationships, our *negative thoughts* and *beliefs* really trip us up as they build one upon the other. However, the most harmful filters, which our "unhelpful" (and that's putting it blandly) misperceptions are seen through, are the first and foremost assumptions we make about our very own selves called *Core False Identities*. We think those false identities are **us,** our actual identities. At our core we believe that these erroneously formed assumptions are truly who we are. This is what Bella Divina meant in that shocking revelation on the road… "And these identities reside within you."

We are physical and energetic expressions of the Pure Potentiality of Love. False Identities are really distortions in our energy field (that mind-body-spirit connection within us; that electro-magnetic "soup" of us.) They're caused by our unresolved negative beliefs and their consequent emotions.

Think about this for a moment. Imagine an encounter, which you *could* perceive as emotionally painful. Now imagine that you feel neutral about it, rather than hurt — that you are engaged simply as an observer, not only of another person's behavior, but of your own as well. Just an observer, a witness. No judgment and no taking anything personally.

And just imagine, a little further, of being in this encounter in a state of curiosity, simply thinking to yourself, "Isn't this interesting?" Or even participating in the encounter in a state of love. Being in a space of unshakeable love — of you, of the other person, of what *is* — simply "being love" no matter what. Your ego will smack you up side your head and keep screaming, "What's the matter with you?! Why aren't you fighting back? You weak son of a gun! Let 'em have it!!" Etc., etc., etc. And, yet, you would still choose to "be love."

Now that's a challenge if there ever was one. AND a potentiality worth reaching for. It **is** possible. It is what we can evolve into, if we choose to.

There are about 7-plus billion perspectives of love in the world today. Why? Because love means something unique and exquisitely personal to each and every human being alive. A person's history, and their interpretations of that history, color their perception. Every hope, heartache, disappointment and *unmet* need creates a theory of love. Every *met* need, every act of kindness and smile meant for them, every expression of caring about them goes into a description of love.

We typically view love as something to give and something to get, but ultimately love comes from within us. Biologically speaking, it is said that the brain is our biggest sex organ, and to a very large degree that is true. Our heart, as you will see, is bigger still. And these two centers can work in tandem, with intention, towards the greatest love you could ever know.

Esoterically speaking, it is said that we are the manifestors of our lives. And as such, we "invite" people into our lives to play the roles that we assign to them. They "show up" in physical form to assist us in our evolution, as our parents or friends or siblings or co-workers or neighbors or strangers… etc., and we perceive them to be friends or foes.

Things that happen in our lives cause us to create our own unique interpretations and perceptions — never to be experienced in exactly the same way by anyone else. Similar — yes. But exactly — no. How could it be? "Anyone else" was never at that "occurrence," at that precise time, in those same pair of shoes, with the same personality, having had the same parents, teachers and peers, with the same previous learnings, perceptions and conclusions that "You" have.

At the exact moment of any given life event, we choose how we perceive it, experience it, and what to do with it from then on. And this, too, is what we do with our personal interpretations of Love. We feed our thoughts, perceptions, and inner wolves — those intense and powerful emotions — of either love or anger. As the Native American Grandfather in the Introduction shared, "we choose."

It all comes down to this simple question: What do you want? In terms of love in your relationship, what do you want? You, and only you, can answer that for yourself. So answer thoroughly and honestly. The finesse of relationship, then, will be combining, communicating, cooperating and collaborating with the person you have chosen to share this highly unique space with you. It's a space that only the two of you can create — a new reality — given both your histories and your perceptions, and your desires to *relate* and *create* beyond what you both have ever known.

You are the builders of your life together. If you want love and peace in your life, and in your relationship, consider this. The 'brick and mortar' of a loving relationship includes:

- Full Communication — listening as well as talking
- Honesty and Integrity — in all things; especially when it's difficult or scary
- Respect and even Reverence — for oneself and one's beloved
- Acceptance and Understanding — even if one's ego objects
- Appreciation and Affection — genuinely felt and easily given
- Presence — making the relationship a priority
- Forgiveness — of yourself and of your beloved
- Mutuality — not only in chores, but also in creativity and nurturance
- Compassion — awareness of your beloved's suffering and "being there" for them
- Support — emotionally, mentally, spiritually, and physically
- Faithfulness — to the relationship and to the beloved
- And certainly more! What would "more" be for you?

Again, the bottom line is:

What Do You Want?

Go within and find out.
Here's how.

CHAPTER 2

Healing From the Loss of Love

So you've been left, discarded, kicked to the curb. If you've ever heard the words, "I don't love you anymore," they drum consistently in your memory. Maybe those exact words were never spoken, but they screamed out in the silence of no replies. Maybe they were said over and over again by you or your partner until they finally "took." However it went having the life squeezed out of your relationship(s), you're here, now, wanting to heal.

This could be the very first moment of a life that you can and will — if you choose — create as *completely new*. Not a new version of the old stuff, but a brand new life. One you could never have created before because you've not (yet) been in the place of awareness and motivation that you will be in by the time you finish this book.

It's about Energy. The study of this new knowledge is incredibly complex and in its infant stages, but what has been discovered so far is fascinating.

Obviously, we're physical and emotional beings. Just feel your aching heart.

PHYSICALLY

Our bodies have various systems: circulatory, respiratory, limbic, nervous, lymphatic, digestive, endocrine, immune, muscular, reproductive, skeletal, and elimination. Each of the different systems in our bodies has its own intelligence and operational systems — blood, neurons, bones, fluids, etc.

Let's, for a moment, look at the intelligence and field of the heart touched upon in the Introduction. Research by the Institute of HeartMath has documented the interesting relationship of cardiac reactions to different emotional energies. When any of us experiences various emotions, our heartbeat does not necessarily change, but the spaces *between* the beats do. When we're under stress, be it from external forces or internal thoughts, the rhythmic patterns of our heartbeat become disordered, sharp and jagged — just like the rocks on our path. When we experience the emotions of love, care, kindness and compassion, the rhythmic patterns flow in a beautiful, easy sine wave.

Cardiovascular researchers and neurophysiologists have discovered that the heart has its own nervous system, with somewhere in the neighborhood of 40,000 sensory neurites. This nervous system is totally separate from the brain's, and the neurons in the heart can actually **sense**, **feel**, and **remember**.

The heart puts out 2½ watts of power with every heartbeat, creating an electromagnetic field that extends up to 3 feet from the body and is felt even beyond that. The brain's field emits only about one inch beyond its source. The heart's electromagnetic field, **5000** times more powerful than the brain's, extends all around the body — and *every heartbeat broadcasts how we're feeling into that field*. The waveforms in the field communicate with and permeate every cell of our body, and then go out into the world around us. This activity is called "non-local" or "quantum," meaning their influence exists even at a distance.

Similar to the heart and each system of the body, each cell has its own intelligence and field, also non-local or quantum in their effects. The human body, without a doubt, is magnificently designed and brilliantly engineered.

And I use the word 'brilliantly' broadly here. That's because the non-local/quantum feature of our bodily functions, which enables them to communicate amongst each other, is assisted by yet another system called our "energy body." This too has an electromagnetic quality — it's sub-atomic and emitted through photons or light particles, which are devoid of matter or density. Our energy system has enormous power, which affects the health of both our bodies and our psyches.

According to Donna Eden, a widely-known and respected pioneer in the field of Energy Medicine (and author of the book **Energy Medicine**), "Not only does every person carry a distinguishing energy, so too does every cell, every organ, and every system of the body. Your body carries an intelligence that exceeds the understanding of your intellect. Your energy body is the subtle counterpart of your physical body and it is more responsive than your physical body to many kinds of influences."

So — our energy system operates at a *sub-microscopic level* and is responsible for the flow of life force throughout our bodies! Various cultures have their own names for it. The Chinese call it "Qi," meaning breath, and it's considered the primary principle of all living things. In Hindu Indian culture it's known as "Prana," the word for life.

Energy runs through our bodies via "meridians." Ancient cultures called them "pathways" or "energy rivers" that carried balance and vitality to the major organs throughout the body. Physical and emotional illnesses were thought to be brought about by blockages in these energy rivers. The first written indications of therapeutic interventions in China came from the Shang dynasty of over 4000 years ago. Stone and bone needles were found in tombs from that era, which may have been used for acupuncture. By the 2nd century CE, over 600 points on the body were acknowledged in China as acupuncture sites. And by this same time 20 meridians, or energy rivers, in the body were recognized and charted. The most high-tech tracking system they had 2000 years ago was diagnosis by pulse feeling. A far cry, to be sure, from today's scanning equipment.

Somewhere along the way our Western culture lost touch with the knowledge of energy rivers, but thanks to the advancement of scientific technology, scientists (Pierre de Vernejoul, Dr. Claude Darras, Dr. Hiroshi Motoyma, and countless more) have now been able to detect and graph the locations and structures of meridians, and illustrate the effects of this submicroscopic system. They've opened great doorways of discovery. What we now know thanks to research by Dr. Bjorn Nordenstrom, former chairman of the Nobel Prize committee on medicine, is that a weak current (energy), as a vast electrical system, flows within us, in the interstitial spaces between the cells of the body and in the blood stream as well.

So, what does all of this have to do with Love? (Keep with me here because this stuff is not only fascinating, it can change your life.) Here's how it works.

These meridians and acupuncture points play a role in therapeutic interventions. True. And recently a profound discovery has been made in the field of psychology. We know that subtle energy is ushered through the meridian system, which has specific points of activation known as acupuncture points. With that in mind, the field of Energy Psychology employs the capabilities of meridians in what are known as Meridian Energy Therapies, aka Energy Techniques. These modalities are very simple, yet incredibly effective, in releasing the energies of trauma that have been "stuck" in the body for perhaps years.

By stuck, I really mean stuck — not only emotionally but physiologically. When a trauma, like a break-up, happens there is a whole lot of emotion going on around it. Generally speaking, we don't just break up with someone and then go whistling on our way. There's an emotional kick back to that experience. The energetic effects of the trauma, or emotional "insult" from the experience, imbed themselves in our electromagnetic field, which, as you now realize, extends beyond us. Repressed memories of the trauma are also held in the base brain known as the amygdala, where they loop around and around. And the negative effects of this energy will remain in there until they are released.

Energy Psychology research has shown that the energy created by a trauma, along with its associated feelings, can be released through the Meridian Energy Therapies. Some of the more commonly known Energy Techniques are called "tapping techniques" because, as you will learn, we tap on various acupuncture points to usher out the trapped energy. These energy therapies/modalities/techniques are easy to learn. Once you've gotten the concept, you can use them any place, any time to release emotional suffering, which you'll learn more about later in the book.

Energy Field Disruptions

OUR EXCHANGES WITH OTHERS, as we go through life, give us very valuable feedback concerning what we believe about them and, more importantly, about ourselves. And our intimate relationships provide us with the greatest challenges as well as the greatest growth. Invariably, conflict comes into any love contract. And because the pain is so deep, it is imperative and urgent to transcend the perceptions of our egos — that is, unless we want to keep adding to the fermentation of fury that will grow.

Painful experiences that arise from past conflict are more than just emotional insults. Thoughts of anger or vengeance are more than just thoughts. Beliefs of self-loathing are more than just beliefs. Patterns of behavior such as chronic disorganization, procrastination, withdrawals from social interaction, or other non-productive tendencies are more than they seem to be. These all are *more* than just what happens in the physical moment. These are energy flow problems. If you just sit still long enough to get in touch with the feelings of sadness or anger or grief coursing through your body when these things occur, you'll understand what I mean by energy flow.

Humans are *bio-magnetic* (life-attracting) and *bio-electric* (capable of generating power) beings. Our bodies are an electro-magnetic field, a "region or space" of weakly running circuits of energies, as described by Dr. Bjorn Nordenstrom. When a trauma, disruption, or "insult" occurs, there is an effect not unlike events we experience in the material world.

Consider the squirrel doing its dance on the power line in Ohio that caused the huge power outage affecting the Northeast quadrant of the United States in 2003. Hurricane Sandy in 2012, is another clear example of the enormous effect of disruption and trauma. These catastrophes are akin to what transpires within us energetically when we experience deeply traumatic occurrences in our intimate relationships. At an internal level, love — denied, rejected, or betrayed — is, to us, the energetic equivalent of these disasters.

The traumas of painful beliefs and emotional insults are, at their most basic level, ***energy field disruptions*** that become encoded in the body's limbic system. They then become embedded in the physical body and can become chronic patterns. It's quite a fascinating sequence, similar to what happens to the TV when there is a power snafu. The picture may flicker, turn wavy, turn to static "snow" or go dark. And the perfectly normal program we were viewing becomes aggravatingly defunct.

When a snafu occurs in a person's otherwise normal life, the body's bio-circuitry responds in similar fashion. The muscles of the body will stiffen, and then cortisol and other stress hormones, produce damage. These hormones and even smaller chemicals called neuropeptides, act to lock the feeling of the trauma into the body and mind. From there, chronic patterns or symptoms can develop.

Physically the person might begin to develop "knots" in their stomach, neck, shoulders or back, or in their muscles in general. Vague un-wellness or even overt illness might set in. If there is no intervention the person is at risk of chronic deterioration taking hold. Emotionally, similar risk is possible. The person might develop maladaptive emotional tendencies such as depression, anger management challenges, or a Victim mentality, along with other faulty thinking. If there is no intervention, emotional deterioration continues.

Emotional or energetic upsets, actual or perceived, give rise to and perpetuate deeply held negative beliefs, which then give rise to the inaccurate conclusions we formulate about ourselves — our Core False Identities (which you will learn more about in later chapters.) These Identities seek sustenance from whatever events or circumstances they can feed off of in the cycle of their re-creation. And from there they can cause utter havoc in not only our own lives, but in the lives of those who are even near us in proximity.

I'd like to share a story to illustrate what I mean.

A few years ago, while traveling in Africa with my friends, Karen and Tom, we stayed in a lovely, classy resort at the top of the Zambian side of Victoria Falls. Our meals were in a restaurant separately located from lodging. On our maiden trek to the restaurant, meandering down the outdoor walk, we passed by giraffes and zebras, all kinds of wildly-horned animals (just beyond a barely visible mesh fence), birds of every color known to man, and probably slithery, crawly things that we mercifully did not encounter.

At every meal the staff members warned us not to take any food back to our rooms because of the "naughty monkeys." These naughty monkeys would come out of nowhere, jump on people and steal the food right out of their hands as they were walking down the path to their buildings. We also were told to keep our front doors (which opened out to the beautifully manicured property) and our sliding glass doors (which opened out to a view of the mightily flowing Zambezi River just before it threw itself over the cliffs) locked. Not just closed tightly, but locked. Guess why?

These monkeys would enter vulnerable rooms and ransack them. One woman was actually resting on her bed enjoying the thin sliver of a breeze coming into her room, when a band of the critters started prying the unsecured sliding door open. In her hysterics, she screamed and clubbed them away, curtains flying everywhere.

Unfortunately my friends did not hear the "locked" part of our instructions, and one day when we went to visit the spectacular falls, the monkeys paid a call. Upon our return, Tom and Karen found utter destruction in their once lovely room.

The monkeys had gone straight for the wet bar and broken all the bottles open to drink the contents — there was shattered glass everywhere. They opened every packet of sugar and ate the granules. They ate the snack packages in the wet bar drawers. Or at least the ones they liked — the others they just smooshed into the carpet or threw against the walls. They got into Karen's purse on the chair and flung all its contents around the room. Their suitcases were stomped on and contents dumped. The gorgeous bed linens were tossed into heaps. Anything paper was shredded. Lamps were tipped over and lampshades were bashed.

This is a point that's really, really important to remember. Our negative core beliefs are like "naughty monkeys." They're not frivolous. They're not harmless. They're not just thoughts we "play around with" in our minds. They are enormously destructive. And they **will** jeopardize the journey of a person's life — and maybe take down a few innocent bystanders in the process.

What do I mean? Here's the end of the story.

Not knowing what had happened in my friends' room until later, I was gazing outside my sliding doors at the gorgeous landscape. I noticed the trees just in front of our rooms were being blown around like we were in the middle of a hurricane — even though I saw wind nowhere else. It looked so odd to see the branches of the trees that were inert less than a minute before being shaken and twisted so violently. I looked around the grounds and saw that no other trees were affected. So I looked closer — it was the monkeys. They were absolutely insane — jumping in and out of the trees, racing all over the grounds as though on fire. It was a frenzied, frantic scene. These were not happy animals — they were crazed animals. I wondered about what would have happened to anyone who entered into the frenzy. No one dared. We all stayed behind our glass doors.

This is what our negative beliefs, and especially our Core False Identities, do. They translate into erratic, if not destructive, behavior. Anyone in our way can get hurt, even if it was never our intention. And people instinctively know to keep their distance.

But our bodily cells, however, cannot. Our cells comprise the physical form of us and are at the effect of our thoughts and beliefs. They do not escape the devastation of the rampage.

In the world of nature, after animals survive traumatic ordeals (like running for their lives), they literally stop and shake their bodies to within an inch of the life they just nearly lost. Yes, that hard. They shake from their core, as though to rid themselves of peripheral body parts. And they continue to shake, and shake some more, until they are done. "Done" meaning that the effects of the horrific scare have left their body.

We humans don't do that. Instead, our traumas take residence in our bodies. They become stockpiled, and wreak havoc with the fight or flight aspect of our nervous system. It's a dilemma and a vicious cycle. And unfortunately, relationships are the primary place where the scariest confrontations and deepest hurts happen.

Fortunately for us, we now have Energy Psychology techniques such as EFT (Emotional Freedom Technique) and RITT (Rapidly Integrated Transformation Technique) to assist us in neutralizing our negative thoughts and beliefs. These techniques fall under the category of Acupressure

Therapies (aka: Meridian Therapies or Energy Techniques), which means that acupressure/acupuncture points located at specific sites on the body are gently stimulated by tapping them or simply holding them. This activity also can reduce pain, relax the heart rate and turn off that response. Switching off the fight-or-flight response reduces the stress of the emotions caused by self-sabotaging beliefs. Reducing the effects of those negative beliefs can then lead towards the cultivation of greater self-empowerment.

What this means for human beings is that the energy of the trauma from past hurts, which lodges in the body for sometimes many years, can be released through EFT and RITT, which in turn helps us move on to a sense of well-being, more peace, and greater productivity.

The pain and suffering of our False Identities goes so deep I wouldn't be surprised that it goes back into past lifetimes, if there are such things. That's how deeply, deeply, deeply we are affected. Our life force is seriously compromised by our faulty thinking, plain and simple.

CHAPTER 4

Our Energy Companions Along the Road

WE ALL GET INTO TROUBLE by something called "Victim Thinking." It's operational in each of us as a construct of our ego, under the guise of self-protection. What better way to keep us away from the dangers of "out there" than by infiltrating our thoughts and beliefs with imagined possible harm? If fear doesn't keep us safe from harm by keeping us stagnant, then our resident "Victim" will make sure we don't jump into the danger pool again.

Note to Self: Ego and Victim are not "bad." Ego is just doing its job, and Victim is just one of the tools of the trade.

Take little Johnny for example. He's such the social butterfly in kindergarten and hasn't quite got school etiquette down yet — no disruptive talking, always listen to the teacher, no distracting noises, remain in your seat, etc. Things like that.

So Johnny gets a new Power Ranger — his very favorite toy in the world — and just has to show it to his friend Timmy. The two begin to play with this amazing new toy. Enter the teacher. Johnny didn't even see her coming, and was completely startled by the verbal punishment that ensued. His first thought was, "What did I do? I'm just sharing with my best friend. Why is my nice, sweet teacher yelling at me? I must be bad." At that moment, in his shock and terror, little Johnny locked a trauma into his body. In that moment he unconsciously decided that even nice, sweet people will turn on you, so you'd better not trust *anybody!* You're not safe anywhere, not even when you're doing nice things like sharing. School is not a safe place. Life is not safe. On and on his thinking went, unknowingly setting all these decisions in stone in his little boy brain.

It stayed with him wherever he went. Over the years Johnny dragged his little boy decisions with him into his life as an adolescent, and then on into adulthood. He did not trust people. Period. He stayed on the sidelines of life and protected his scared-of-people self by living an isolated existence. This is Victim Thinking. And this is what Energy Modalities can *neutralize and release* from Johnny's psyche and body. And from yours.

ARCHETYPES WE SHARE

Caroline Myss is an international speaker and writer in the fields of health, energy medicine, medical intuition, human consciousness and spirituality. She has devoted her work to the study of emotional, psychological and spiritual avenues of health. Many of her books in the field of Energy Anatomy connect the dots between emotional, psychological and spiritual stress patterns and physical disease. Myss, a *New York Times* bestselling author and public speaker, claims in her book **Sacred Contracts** that there are four universal archetypes that all human beings have in common: the Child, the Saboteur, the Prostitute, and the Victim. She calls these archetypes our "four principal energy companions."

Simply put, archetypes are neutral energy patterns that we operate from in physical life. They are neither good nor bad. Just neutral. We can usually pinpoint the energy of any archetype in just one word. For example, if I were to say "King" you would instantly know the energy I am trying to convey. You may have a different physical perception of a king than I or anyone else might, but the image of "King" connotes a man of power and majesty. If you heard the word "Slave" you would have an instant perception of a person with no power.

The four energies of Child, Saboteur, Prostitute, and Victim exist as energy patterns in each and every one of us. They show us our opportunities for spiritual strength as we face our challenges, and they reveal how we "give away our power" through our fears. And this is how they do it, according to Myss:

The Child: "The Guardian of Innocence."
The Child's core issue is that of growing up. We learn when and how to shed the comfort of our dependency and move into awareness and responsibility. We learn to discern healthy

dependency from an unhealthy sense of responsibility or unearned guilt. The role of *The Child* is to help us heal and put an end to our own inner self-abuse, to identify what nurtures and inspires us, and to initiate a relationship with our 'self' that is caring.

The Prostitute: The Guardian of Faith

The Prostitute's core issue is about how much you will sell yourself out. And which pieces will you sell? "Your morals, your integrity, your intellect, your word, your body, or your soul?" When our survival is threatened we will abandon any or all of these. *The Prostitute's* path is in learning how to take care of oneself, and knowing that "the Divine is looking out for you." When we operate through the power of that faith, then we no longer feel the need to sell pieces of our soul to buy safety.

The Saboteur: The Guardian of Choice

The Saboteur's core issue is the fear of "inviting change into your life, change that requires responding in a positive way to opportunities to shape and deepen your spirit." It deals with the questions: Why do I resist opportunities for happiness or success? Why do I not take responsibility for myself and for what I create? *The Saboteur* offers to us the invitation to listen to that inner spiritual voice, follow our intuition, act with courage and use our power to change our lives. Or not.

The Victim: The Guardian of Self-Esteem

The Victim invites us to look honestly at our relationship with power (especially in our dealings with people who seek to control or dominate us), and to set boundaries that will honor our safety and self-respect. *Victim* is universal to every human being and "may manifest the first time you don't get what you want or need…or are accused of or punished for something you didn't do… But at a certain point you discover a perverse advantage to being the Victim. The core issue of the Victim is whether it's worth giving up your own sense of empowerment to avoid taking responsibility for your independence."

Like Johnny did.

Myss's perspective is that "each archetype is a 'face' and 'function' of the Divine that manifests within each of us individually."

How strange to think of our Victim as a "face" and "function" of the Divine, and yet it is. Our Victim shows us the twisted journey to our soul's liberation. The greatest, and perhaps harshest, journey is our quest for Love. While its path first appears as lovely and glistening as a peaceful river at sunrise, it will at times become a painful, twisted torrent of heartache — and possibly *heartbreak*. If we choose to learn and grow from our navigation of this journey, and if we stay faithful to the process, we will find more than safety and refuge. At the end of the journey, if we choose to take it, is something of a big and beautiful surprise.

Let's talk about this path.

It's a strange and daunting road, this path of Love, full of obstacles and pitfalls, which you will come to know as negative beliefs and false identities. We think the people who stand in our way are the problems we are to overcome in our march out of victimhood and into love. We think the people who push at our egos are our victimizers.

And there are those who quite likely think the same of us.

A very crowded path it is. And we're all simply distracting one another from the real problems — OUR VERY OWN PERSONAL BELIEFS — that we're all tripping over.

In our travels down the road, we get banged up a bit and bleed quite a lot. It feels as though the pain we experience comes right from our very heart. It's painful to see life through the eyes of our Victim. And we fall a lot. Into depression, into anger, into vengeance, and more. If we remain unaware, this can cause some serious damage.

The Law of Resonance

HERE'S THE DANGER OF Victim Thinking. As you already know, we are electro-magnetic beings. We each have our own unique frequencies and vibrations. As such, we have resonance.

The Law of Resonance states that when one vibratory system comes into contact with another, the system with the less pronounced vibration will adjust its energy to match the energy of the more pronounced system.

Just think of tuning forks — those double-pronged steel forks that vibrate at a constant pitch when activated, usually by being struck by a metal rod. They have a very pure resonant tone and for that reason they're used to perfectly tune musical instruments. When you twang (not an official word) a tuning fork into tone and then bring a second, perfectly silent tuning fork near it, the silent one will pick up the vibration of the sound. Then when you move the first fork away from the second one, the second fork will, on its own, keep the vibration of the original sound. This is resonance.

Or, think of dialing into your favorite radio channel. If you are close but not precisely aligned with the station's frequency numbers, you will get weak reception, static, or no reception at all. Only when you are on the exact frequency will you clearly hear the sound of the station. This is resonance.

The Law of Resonance is true for us, too, because of our electro-magnetic qualities.

We emit different frequencies at certain levels of power (which will be explained in a later chapter). And the quality, frequency, and strength of the energy we project (put out there) will be picked up by those who come into our energetic field. This certainly gives new meaning to the warning "watch your thoughts."

This is why it was so critical for Tender Heart to clean her rocks and boulders. And it's why we, too, *must* clean, or "clear," our negative thoughts and core beliefs. They're energetically viable — they add to the airwaves, so to speak. They're apparent in the looks on our faces, in the way we walk, in the words we speak, and in the actions that we take. When someone comes into our vibrational field, he/she picks up on the "vibes" we're putting out, and the choice is made to either join in with us, resonating at that level, or turn away to resonate with someone else's more enjoyable "radio station."

Hmm.

And consider the electromagnetics of the heart, which you were introduced to earlier. When we participate in negative thinking, we cause stress in our body, which causes the heartbeat rhythm to be very disordered and discordant. When we choose positive thoughts and beliefs, our heart wave rhythm is orderly and coherent. If you remember from Chapter 2, every heart rhythm waveform is transmitted to every cell in the body. This affects our hormones, our immune system, our perceptions, AND the people around us.

Get this. Research has shown that the pattern of our heart rhythm can show up in the **brain waves**, *(in the exact pattern)* of the people who are only a few feet from us. Talk about Resonance!

There is a communication established within our body between the heart and the brain. The brain needs to align with the intelligence of the heart in order to fulfill its highest purpose. When the brain and heart are out of synch some cortical shutdown occurs. A few of the effects of this are:

We won't be able to see the "bigger picture."
We're more "fear based" in our perceptions and reactions.
We'll attract more incoherence into our life.

The single most important relationship in our lives is the one we have with our very own "Self." Aligning our heart and our head is of paramount importance in this relationship. This alignment amplifies the power of our heart's coherence in the space around us as we interact with the greater field in which we exist.

As you recall from earlier in the book, the heart's electromagnetic field transmits up to three feet beyond us. The field of our energy system extends beyond that. Have you ever felt a connection with someone "across a crowded room?" Perhaps even an auditorium? Have you ever felt that someone was watching you from somewhere, then you turned around to look and saw that their eyes averted from yours a little too late? Have you ever thought about someone and a few minutes later they just happened to call you? This is energy.

The power of our heart's intelligence and our body's energy system combine as such a force that we, indeed, stand as the creators of our lives. Positively or negatively.

When we dwell on, or in, our negative thoughts and/or emotions all we have to do is sit and wait for the negative consequences to come. Because they will — in one form or another. So do you see the necessity (and urgency) in clearing yourself of the energy of your damaging thoughts and beliefs?

C H A P T E R   6

The Makings of Your Story

SINCE *NOW* IS ALWAYS the right time, let's begin to neutralize your core issues. If you've been on a rocky road to Love you won't have to stay on it much longer. Your mission, if you choose to accept it, is this:

Go get your journal, or a piece of paper, or scrap paper, or napkin — if that's all you have — and start writing. Collect all the "**rocks**" you can remember. Recall some of the **negative thoughts** you've held concerning specific people in your life. And, yes, feel free to include Higher Self or Universe or Mind or God, or whatever name you have for that power greater than you.

Just jot down your list of "rocks" — the negative thoughts you've harbored against your mother, father, siblings, teachers and other authority figures, friends, co-workers, bosses, neighbors, lovers, children, strangers, foreigners, people who scared you because they were different, and anyone else you can think of.

See if you can collect 100 negative thoughts. It doesn't matter how insignificant, catty or embarrassing they seem. List any hurtful thoughts you hold. Because you do indeed hold them, not only in your mind but also in your body. It may take you several minutes or a few days. Just do it. At least so you can get this list done.

You may notice that a thought might be repeated, perhaps in different ways. This is a general indicator that **that** perception, in all its variations, is a big deal for you. Keep going until you reach 100 because what happens as you go on is that you begin to reach the more deeply buried subconscious thoughts — the ones you might not have even known you were holding on to. When you're finished, get a sense of how those thoughts have affected you. As you look at the list of thoughts you then will be able to decipher the negative core beliefs (those big boulders) you've formed about others.

When you've completed your **rocks / negative thoughts** list, start to formulate your own personal lists of your larger **boulders / negative core beliefs** — your beliefs about life, men, women, and relationships. These are the bigger issues for you — these issues have caused you pain great enough that you react by judging others, before they can judge or hurt you. They are named *negative CORE beliefs* for a reason. Because they hit you at the deepest level where you live.

Your lists might begin with:

Men are ________________________________.
(List everything you believe about men, no matter
how many pages or napkins it takes.)

Women are ________________________________.
(Again. List, list, list no matter how much paper
you need.)

Relationships are ________________________________.
(You know the drill.)

Life is ________________________________.
(Write your perspectives on life. Good, bad, ugly,
or indifferent.)

The all-important list — YOU — we will save for a
later chapter.

After your lists are as complete as you can make them
at this time, you will begin to clean them like Tender Heart
cleaned her rocks.

Now let's change the story.

Changing Your Story

EVERYTHING WE'VE EXPERIENCED in our lives, and all the thoughts and feelings we have about those experiences, create the story we tell ourselves about ourselves. But we can change the story — not the events as they occurred, but the thoughts and feelings we carry around as a result.

I've already mentioned two Energy Techniques that can help. Emotional Freedom Technique (EFT) is the most widely known — I call it the Mother Ship of our contemporary tapping techniques. If you're unfamiliar with these techniques, chances are the first one you'd hear about is EFT. It's quite well recognized these days. The other modality is, as of yet, less known but is coming into the foreground. It is called the Rapidly Integrated Transformation Technique (RITT). While similar to EFT, it adds a further component which you will read about later.

In both techniques you will be tapping, very lightly, with a couple of your fingers, on certain acupuncture/acupressure points on your body. Don't worry about the where and when — it's all spelled out for you in Appendix A and Appendix B.

But first a little history about EFT.

Gary Craig, a Stanford engineer, is the creator of EFT, which is based on a technique known as Thought Field Therapy (TFT). TFT was created by Dr. Roger Callahan, referred to as the "Founder of Energy Tapping."

In 1981, Dr. Callahan — a highly successful psychologist — was absolutely stymied by a water phobia afflicting his patient, "Mary." It was so severe, she was even terrified of baths. He'd tried everything he knew to help her and none of it seemed to work in any measurably significant way. As a final attempt, he elected to combine traditional psychology with what he knew about the meridian system. He had Mary tap under her eye (the acupressure point for fear) as she talked about her incapacitating terror. Within moments, she reported that the fear had disappeared.

Mary, in her delight, went outside to the pool in the back area and began wading in the shallow end. Dr. Callahan was a little disconcerted by this and nervously called out to her that he was pretty uncomfortable about the situation. Mary's retort was, "Don't worry, Doctor. What we just did took my fear away — it didn't make me stupid." From that single session, Mary no longer suffered from her phobia.

Callahan was blown away by this, and dedicated his career to developing this new system of psychology/acupuncture therapy, which he labeled "Thought Field Therapy" (TFT).

His system is a compilation of many different "tapping codes" or algorithms (step by step procedures). It basically combines talking about your anger, grief, or fear (or whatever is bothering you), while gently tapping certain acupuncture points.

Gray Craig, a very motivated student of TFT, refined and simplified this process, and went on to devote his life to making EFT freely available to the general public. In this technique you simply tap on the same points, but don't need to follow complicated algorithms. This tapping technique is used to treat deep-seated grief, fear, anger, and trauma such as PTSD (Post-Traumatic Stress Disorder). One of the great things about EFT is that you don't need to talk about your problem until the cows come home. You can simply recall a memory or an emotion and start tapping.

One grateful practitioner at a time, the world is learning to transform its pain through EFT. It's simple, immediately utilizable, and it's life changing.

For this practice just follow the guidelines in Appendix A.

CLEANING YOUR ROCKS

My advice would be to use EFT to process and release the emotional charge you feel about the items on your 100 negative thoughts list. EFT is so simple, yet so very effective at neutralizing the energy, that these thoughts can be "cleared" of their charge quite quickly. And let's face it, 100 is not a small number.

If you're the kind of person who has no intention of doing this, I get it. I was there once. Just know it's your ego that's resisting. Your soul may want relief, but your ego is screaming, "No!" Just continue reading.

If you do want to neutralize the discomfort of some of your thoughts, here's where you begin. Use your list of **Negative Thoughts / Rocks** as practice to get used to EFT and the experience of tapping. Pick the thoughts that really stand out for you (they usually are first on the list, or they may have occurred later after generating momentum in your memories). The point is, deal with the prominent thoughts first, just in case you lose steam — any minor issues will very likely be cleared by your work with the major thoughts.

Now, here's what you do:

Have Appendix A open in front of you so you can follow it. You may feel awkward at first. You might worry that you're doing it wrong. Not to worry. There's no way you can do it wrong if you follow the directions. After a while it will all become second nature to you. Before long, you'll find yourself relaxing into it so much that you'll be more fluid about the wording and begin to put your own personal style into the process.

The idea is to get in touch with the feelings you have around the memories that come up. You can swear; you can cry; you can simply feel the emotion. Or you can just say the words and tap on the points with no feeling at all. Whatever is real for you and whatever happens is okay, correct, and good. The tapping will release any discomfort, as you do the process. The memory will remain, but the emotional pain or charge around it will become neutralized.

To begin, read a negative thought that you have listed and feel into the emotion connected to the thought. If you have a specific memory connected to the thought, allow yourself to remember it. Then, on a scale of 1 to 10 (with 1 being the least and 10 being the most) rate your discomfort. Give a number indicating the intensity of feeling that you have. Most people start somewhere near 8, 9, or 10. The reason you do this is to be able to assess how much the discomfort has subsided after you do a "round" of tapping. You will repeat this rating after each round.

A "round" constitutes the tapping sequence from the crown to the liver points. The goal is to get to zero discomfort. Zero means that you no longer have any "charge" or trauma about the issue. Sometimes it takes up to 3 rounds of tapping in order to reach that zero. If you don't get to zero, it's okay. You can always do EFT at a later time.

In the event that 3 rounds didn't do the trick and you want to continue, then you would do the 9 Gamut Sequence. It's pretty uncommon that anyone has to use it, but it's included for you in Appendix A, just in case.

Ready??

Take the first **Negative Thought / Rock** on your list and follow the directions for EFT laid out for you in Appendix A. When finished with that item (meaning that you've reached zero charge), cross it off your list. Move on to the next one. When that feels cleared from any charge, move on to the next. Clear and move on, etc., etc., etc.

You will find that as you clean one "rock" some other "rocks" will be cleaned as well. It happens quite often that when one item is cleared of its charge, other similar or related items will be neutralized as well. So if you get to a later item on your list and no longer have any charge about it, just know it was cleared already and gratefully cross it off your list. Try not to be delighted (I'm kidding!) when several beliefs drop all of their charge after one single previous clearing.

CLEARING YOUR NEGATIVE CORE BELIEFS

Now move on to your **Negative Core Beliefs /Boulders** list. These are the larger and more painful beliefs you hold about men, women, relationships, and life. These perceptions you really want to neutralize. Why? Because they're holding you back — from enjoyment, perhaps from success, from growth, and certainly from liberation. You, no doubt, have very valid reasons for harboring these beliefs. (Soon we'll look at the Cycle of Re-Creation, which will explain how your beliefs were developed.)

As with Negative Thoughts, the first few boulders on your Negative Core Beliefs list are usually the most prominent in your psyche. So, again, this is where you start clearing. Once again you can use EFT. By now you have experienced how effective it is.

Just go at it. Your desire for relief will determine how many beliefs you clear, which ones you clear, or *if* you want to clear them. You are in charge here. All I can tell you is that when we get to that all-important person — YOU — you are probably going to want to be as clear of this other stuff as you possibly can.

So get out your Negative Core Beliefs list and go for it.

CHAPTER 8

The Cycle of Re-Creation

Because Core False Identities, the "hoodoos" that reside within us, are so important to discover and acknowledge, let's keep investigating, shall we?

How did we get these false identities? Well, we cultivated something called our very own unique "Cycle of Re-Creation." Very early on in life, before we were even aware of it, we developed certain beliefs about ourselves. Then as life continued, some demoralizing encounters happened that we thought proved our beliefs to be true. We took it at face value, shrugged our shoulders in resignation, and basically said to ourselves, "See? I really am a schmuck (or whatever other term we use)."

In our Cycle of Re-Creation, we subconsciously re-create, draw to us, and "fall victim to" relationship conflicts in our lives that seemingly substantiate the *original beliefs* we formed about ourselves. These conflicts appear as happenstance, but they actually were subconsciously set up by us. Haven't you ever found yourself saying "Why does this always happen to me?" It happens because our thoughts and our actions placed us at the scene.

I know this is hard to swallow, but this is how it works:

These upsets or insults came into our relationships by our actions and reactions, basically our **choices,** which *created* the circumstances which took place. Let me say this a little more simply. Our actions and reactions to whatever life has brought us, and the choices we've made that were set in motion by those actions/reactions, led up to and created the present scenario we are in. This all goes back in time a very long way. And this is how it goes down.

Somehow or another we find ourselves in a conflict with another person. Because of this clash we are triggered. We're hopping mad — but NOT so much by the argument itself. We're triggered by a belief about ourselves that surfaced because of the altercation. This is a belief we're not all that conscious about, but subconsciously we've held on to it painfully for a long, long time — maybe most of our life. The present conflict seems to confirm that this belief about ourselves is actually true.

Conflicts are basically disagreements. If someone doesn't agree with us our immediate reaction comes in the form of "How dare you… Jerk!" But it's really not about them. They're just stating another point of view; their point of view. In actuality we are triggered by the belief that we're inadequate, that we're "less than," and we are being "found out" by not being right. After all (says the old belief inside us), if we're not "right" then what good are we?

We want to think that we are adequate, that we know the exact right thing, the truth, the details, etc. Maybe we feel disregarded or stupid or disrespected or insignificant by what the other person said or did. The truth is, if we didn't already believe we were inadequate, or insignificant or "less than", then what they said, or did, wouldn't have even registered as an affront.

Do you disagree with me?

Here's an example: if someone told you that you had antlers growing out of your head, you'd simply think that comment was peculiar, or maybe even intriguing. You might even chuckle at the idea. It wouldn't bother you because you knew it wasn't true. In like manner, if we really believed that we were enough or significant then a person's disagreeing with us wouldn't bother us. It would only be fodder for fascinating conversation. They and we may never agree, but we might come up with a radically brilliant solution.

When we are triggered in a conflict, we think it's the other person's fault. And we blame *them*. But in reality, it's our "original wound," — and the misperceptions we formed about ourselves because of that first wound — that are being brought up. In reality, it's about the choices we've made all along to carry that emotional wound up to the present conversation.

This is how the Cycle of Re-Creation works. We keep re-creating "evidence" that we're flawed, wrong, inept, and worthless…until such time as we **choose** to decide that "evidence" is unsubstantiated and untrue.

I think an example might be helpful here. Let's take a look at Tender Heart's Cycle of Re-Creation

Take out a piece of white drawing paper, 8.5"x11" and place it on the table. Draw a circle; it doesn't have to be perfect. Now, draw a small stick figure at the top of the circle (If you envision the circle as a clock — 12:00) Make sure the stick figure is small enough to visually express the sheer tininess of the individual next to the hugeness of the outside world, but big enough so we can tell that this is a living, breathing human being. Think of all the blankness on the white paper as pure potentiality or the "blank slate" — how we all enter the world.

The stick figure at the top of that large circle is a newborn Tender Heart. She's a happy little baby, with her whole life ahead of her. Now draw a curved arrow outside of the circle, down to 2:00, and stop. What we're doing is following the path of her life with the curved arrows you'll keep drawing outside the arc of the circle.

At 2:00 Tender Heart, still a baby, sees life as peaceful and good. There's only one problem — she wasn't a great napper. She didn't like being put away in the crib — suffering the boredom and loneliness of naptime, and the indignity of still being trapped, despite her crying for release when naptime was over. "Why will no one come get me?" Her little Self began to feel that no one wanted to listen to her calling for help, and it was only one of her first "evidences" of the belief that she wasn't worth caring about. And in addition, there were the wet diapers, nobody to hold her, pent up unattended burps…

These are the first rocks Tender Heart placed on the path she will eventually walk. Right now they're only subconscious, but soon enough they'll trip her up.

Let's continue the curved arrows. Draw an arc outside the circle another couple of inches and end it with your arrowhead. We'll call this 4:00.

By the time the arrow you draw on the circle goes to about 4:00, Tender Heart is 2 years old and pretty darn tired of the whole procedure. There often was no one to give her toys that lay outside of her reach, nobody to pick her up when her beginner legs crumpled her to the floor, veggies on her plate when she wanted blueberry buckle, dreaded naptime… I could continue ad nauseam here, but you get the message. As life goes by she will continue to find more "evidence" to prove this belief as true: "No one really cares about me."

More rocks and probably a boulder or two (parents, and perhaps siblings.)

When the arrow gets to 6:00, she's in school. Tender Heart is very shy, so the teacher just lets her be that way — never calling on her. And the kids found friends in each other, but didn't include her. (Except for Charlotte who became her single best friend.)

Rocks and boulders everywhere at school, except for Charlotte.

Remember…this is Tender Heart's perspective. We don't know why the teacher didn't call on her a lot. Maybe she was super smart and the teacher, knowing this, elected to exercise the other students' brains. Maybe the kids wanted her in the group but were intimidated. We don't know.

By the time the arrow goes to 8:00ish, Tender Heart is in high school and still quiet. Charlotte chose a different high school to attend and, so of course, didn't really care about being with **her** during those all-important girlfriend years.

Tender Heart was still subconsciously collecting data that her beliefs were the truth about her. The truth could be that Charlotte's parents couldn't afford the same school and had to send Charlotte to another one. And as it generally happens, friends drift away into other friendships.

Oops. There goes Charlotte into the rock and boulder pile, along with her parents.

The arrow goes to 10:00 and Tender Heart is in college. She came out of her shell enough to meet a boy. Life was wonderful for a while. But since he was two years ahead of her, their romance went the way of fizzle as he joined the corporate world in a far-away city. She was crushed, and now convinced, that she was a complete 'loser'; and **in no way was she worth being with or being cared about.**

More hurtful "truth" of her lack of value to anyone in the world.

Her poor boyfriend. He is one mighty big boulder!

So, Tender Heart did what we all do. At a subconscious level we come to conclusions, early on and all along, about ourselves. And then we go through life looking for the evidence that our conclusions are, **in fact**, true.

In fact — cold, hard **fact** — what is true is only that "something" happened. Objectively speaking, all that happened in these brief vignettes of Tender Heart's life are:

Crying baby is put in crib. Mother cleans the house.

Then:
Girl grows up and goes to school. Many kids are playing, and she has 1 friend.
Then:
Boy and girl meet. Have particular encounters.
Boy and girl go separate ways.

If we were to look from 30,000 miles above as some galactic being would, who doesn't have the first inkling what humans are about, that's what we would see. Beings or bodies or things that bump into each other; interact with each other; and leave each other to go do other things, or bump into other beings or bodies or things. It's the **stories** that humans tell themselves about events in their lives that contain the judgments, and consequently the *suffering* in their experiences.

It just gets heavier and heavier, that awful "truth" which just really is not true. One day, if Tender Heart is lucky, she will no longer be able to stand how she feels. And that day might be quite painful, manifesting in a divorce or sickness or other losses. It may be a day that lasts a year… or more. It may last an instant. But that day of reckoning is the day of new birth, a yet uncharted process of growing into a brand new life. It may be confounding, while at the same time being exciting. One thing for sure — it's worth it. And so is she.

The rest of the circle remains for her transformation to occur. Will she do it? Will she see as clearly as we do that her beliefs about herself were inaccurate? That other peoples' choices didn't mean they didn't care about her?

Will she see how her narrow perspective about the motives of others has restricted her enjoyment of life? Will she learn to reframe her thoughts?

Embrace Your Power

PEOPLE DO WHAT PEOPLE DO, for whatever reasons they have to do what they do. They're simply acting from their own set of core beliefs and identity issues derived from their own history. What is *not* helpful for us is to stay **stuck** in the perception that they acted against us because there was something wrong with us. Why? Because that perception puts all of our power "out there". What on earth does that mean?

If we judge and shame ourselves, or immerse ourselves in chronic anger, based on what other people do, then we will forever be at the mercy of other people. **We have absolutely no control about what they think and how they behave.** Furthermore, the anger we aim at them, and the shame we steep ourselves in, fills our heart and energy fields with distorted and incoherent wave patterns that are unhealthy for us, and emit to those around us.

Let's use Tender Heart as an example.

Set into a crib when she was far from interested in napping, and then not rescued until way too late (according to her schedule), Tender Heart's emotions ranged from anger to sadness and maybe a little despair. Other people let her down and at an unconscious level she was foot-stomping mad at them for the control they had, and the neglect she felt. That's usually where we all start. We believe other people are at fault when our needs don't get met.

During her school years Tender Heart suffered some pretty big losses — group acceptance, her best friend, her boyfriend. She continually found "data" that seemingly substantiated her being the loser she'd always felt herself to be. "Loser" is only **one** word she, no doubt, used to define herself. Let's collectively shudder to think what the other words would be. And we *are* entitled to shudder because we've *all* used those words on ourselves.

In these oh so very few events mentioned in Tender Heart's Cycle of Re-Creation, her tendency to blame and self-shame is evident. To be sure, these are only snapshot examples of the self-denigration she's put herself through countless times.

If you're this far into this book, it's obvious you're serious about navigating your life an easier way. The path may start out a little rough, but certainly no rougher than what you've already been going through internally. All you'll be doing is bringing forth what's been held inside of you so you'll be conscious of it, transform it, and move into the amazing world you'd hoped existed — one that you would, if you could, create. You will discover that it does indeed exist — exactly the way you will design it.

The only power we have lies in what goes on within us, and then how we behave from there. So as best as you can, let go of the perspective that others have "done unto you" and be in a place of neutrality. Simply know they are involved with their own complex internal beliefs, and that they're behaving from there. It's simply what is.

Your invitation right now is to look at your Cycles of Re-Creation. Recall incidents in your life that were overtly painful or that covertly left you disliking yourself. Acknowledge some of the beliefs you hold about yourself. This is the pivotal moment of the beginning of your totally new way of "being" in this world. The process does not have to be grueling or scary.

This is not a tool for shaming yourself. Self-shaming is a trick of the ego, or more accurately the super-ego (the super-critical voice inside your head). Shaming holds you in a pit of despair and powerlessness, which is worse than sticky glue to get out of. This pit is unreal — it's only a perception — one that you can choose, or not choose, to hold about yourself.

The despair is real. It's the by-product of the powerlessness that you experience by holding yourself in the contempt of self-shame. Choose instead to see the events, and decisions you made about yourself because of those events, objectively. No judging. Just reporting. Be in a place of curiosity rather than criticism.

This process is designed to elevate you out of your self-judgments. When you see them on paper, you can also see that they are *not* you. They are only the assumptions you inadvertently formed as you plodded through the first few years of your inexperienced life, and then hauled through until now. This one exercise will give you the objectivity you need to initiate the life re-creation for which your heart and soul long.

Tender Heart's circle was a little different from what your process will be here, because hers was used to illustrate many core false beliefs at one time. In reality, we each have many Cycles of Re-Creation — one for each Core False Identity we believe about ourselves. And we would draw one circle, on its own paper, for each individual belief. Who knows? You might collect many pieces of paper or only a few. But for now, start with only one painful belief you hold about yourself. Do it as completely as you can and know that you can always go back and add "events" you might remember later on.

At the top of each circle, instead of the stick figure that signified Tender Heart, write *one* belief you hold about yourself. Then follow your circle around, stopping for every event you recall as having been data that that particular belief is true. Write down all these events as you bring them to mind. The intention is to cite just the big remember-able times that the "evidence" showed up to "prove" you right about your original belief. Write sentences if need be, or just a couple of words if that suffices. This process will really get you in touch with how pervasive that belief has been in your life, the different ways it showed up, and how much it affected you.

For each belief, use a separate sheet of paper and repeat the process.

When we've had enough pain we're motivated to look for a new way to be in this world, so we don't have to experience the suffering anymore. Once you uncover your self-judgments, you will find great joy in dismantling them and replacing them with beliefs that truly serve you.

Consider this message from the Persian poet Rumi.
"Out beyond ideas of wrongdoing and rightdoing there is a field. I'll meet you there."

Concerning your past relationship(s), there is no wrong. There is only what really, really, really did not work.
Love invites you to grow beyond all this.

CHAPTER 10

Hoodoo I Think I Am

AND NOW FOR THE "precision part" of this whole deal. Giving words to the false identities. Distilling judgmental thoughts and negative beliefs about ourselves into what are called "I AM" statements. These are simple, one-liner sentences that capture the essence of what we believe we are. These are **not** the deeper truth of us. They are only judgments we hold about ourselves based on our perceptions.

Tender Heart's statements might be:

I am alone in this world.
I am not worthy.
I am not loved.

They showed up in her life as:
* I'm by myself.
* No one hears me crying.
* No one's coming to get me.
* Teacher won't call on me.
* The other kids don't want to play with me.
* My best friend doesn't even want to be with me.
* The love of my life left me.

"I AM" statements tell it like it has been for us, short and to the point, as they tap into our place of pain. The beauty of doing this precise, albeit painful exercise, is that it quickly gets to the core of what we'd been feeling about ourselves our entire lives.

To help you out, I'd like to share some common False Identities that humanity seems to fall prey to. You may be surprised by what you discover. For the most part, the statements we use to flush the False Identities out begin with the phrase "I AM…" However, due to the concept and the difficulty in wording, there are a few variations.

Again, these statements are meant to show how deeply you have believed yourself to BE these identities. They are NOT the truth of who you are. They are the doorways to your discovery of the deeper truth of You. These false identities…and they truly are false… must first be dis-created so your new creation will begin.

Think of the names you've called yourself. Recall the times you've felt like a victim. How did you feel about yourself?

Now, consider this…this is not about other people and what they "did" to you. This is about You. And what you're doing to yourself. While "their" actions or words caused you pain, what's far more deeply important is the damage you're doing to yourself as a result.

For further enlightenment, throw in the ways you've compared yourself to others. Comparison is an age-old trap of the ego. Measuring ourselves in contrast to another person's abilities will always lead us to believe that one of us is "less than" the other. Usually it's us. Dig deep. The only way out of all this is through it. So throw in comparisons just to be thorough.

Tender Heart, for example, used the words "I'm a loser." Which False Identity speaks the most precisely to that? Perhaps *I'm not loved* or *I don't belong* or *I'm worthless* or *I'm a failure.* What would the word "loser" mean to you? Where would you place it if it were one of your self-beliefs?

Here's a basic list. Underneath the capitalized captions are just a very few ways Core False Identities may show up in life. Think of the ways they really **do** show up for you. Also, you may think of other such Identities and how they show up. Please list them as well. Just remember:

"I am ______________."

I AM ALONE.

This might show up as:
- No one understands me. No one gets me. No one wants me.
- I don't have any support…
- I'm self-sufficient. That way I won't need anyone.

✦ I don't get invited anywhere.
✦ I don't know how to connect.
✦ Your Words:

____

____

I AM NOT SAFE.

This might show up as:
✦ It's a dangerous world out there.
✦ Other people will hurt me.
✦ I have to defend myself.
✦ I'm afraid.
✦ I'm helpless.
✦ Your Words:

____

____

I AM NOT LOVED.
OR
I AM UNLOVABLE

This might show up as:
✦ I feel lost. And no one cares.
✦ Others don't take time to be with me.
✦ Your Words:

____

____

I AM NOT WORTHY.

This might show up as:
- I don't deserve…….
- I'll take care of others so I feel I have value.
- I'll over work, over achieve, over compensate so others won't see I don't have much worth.
- Your Words:

____

____

I AM WORTHLESS/I AM NOT GOOD ENOUGH.

This might show up as:
- I give myself away, either sexually or monetarily, or with my time.
- I'm inadequate.
- I feel like I have no contribution to make in my relationships or community.
- Your Words:

____

____

I AM BAD.

This might show up as:
- I'll be so good that no one will know I'm so bad.
- I'll behave badly so they see that I am bad.
- I'm bad so why should I care about anything.

✦ Your Words:

———————————————————————————

———————————————————————————

I DON'T MATTER.

This might show up as:
- ✦ I'm shy.
- ✦ I don't ask for what I need.
- ✦ People don't care about my needs.
- ✦ Your Words:

———————————————————————————

———————————————————————————

I AM NOT IMPORTANT.

This might show up as:
- ✦ I'm not heard.
- ✦ I'll act like a big deal so others will think I am important.
- ✦ People don't think of me. Or contact me. Or care about me.
- ✦ Your Words:

———————————————————————————

———————————————————————————

I AM NOT ENOUGH.

This might show up as:
- I'll focus on others to the point of sacrificing myself. That way I'll be enough.
- My purpose in life is to please others because they're more important.
- I'm overly responsible and overly considerate.
- Your Words:

____

____

I AM NOT WANTED.

This might show up as:
- They'll reject me.
- If I am who they want me to be, then they'll want me.
- I'm left out.
- Your Words:

____

____

I DON'T BELONG.

This might show up as:
- No place feels right for me.
- I'm living on the outside.
- I would be unwelcome anywhere I go.

✦ Your Words:

____

____

I AM DIFFERENT.

This might show up as:
- I'm a freak, a weirdo.
- There's something wrong with me.
- Your Words:

____

____

I AM INFERIOR.

This might show up as:
- I am a perfectionist.
- I compete to the extreme.
- Others are always better than me.
- Your Words:

____

____

I AM WRONG.

This might show up as:
- It's my fault.

✦ I don't want to make a decision, because I'll make a mistake.
✦ I play small.
✦ Your Words:

____

____

I AM A FAILURE.

This might show up as:
✦ I rarely complete my tasks.
✦ I'm chronically disorganized or messy.
✦ I don't do what I said I would do.
✦ Your Words:

____

____

I AM POWERLESS.

This might show up as:
✦ I'm comfortable being a follower.
✦ I'm weak.
✦ I can't stand up for myself.
✦ I can't say 'no.'
✦ Your Words:

____

____

I AM INVISIBLE.

This might show up as:
  - ✦ No one really sees who I am.
  - ✦ I put my attention on others to the point where I don't even know who I am.
  - ✦ I don't even know what I want or need anymore.
  - ✦ It's like I don't exist.
  - ✦ Your Words:

____

____

When you become clear about how any I AM statement or False Identity shows up for you, it's time to use an energy technique to take the discomfort, or the charge, away. You're already familiar with the process of EFT, which is becoming broadly known. This book contains the classic version crafted by Gary Craig. Second generation versions are coming along now. Coaches such as Nick and Jessica Ortner, Margaret Lynch, Brad Yates (to mention only a few) employ their own variations of EFT, with immense effectiveness.

Also provided for you in this book is another state-of-the-art energy technique known as "RITT" (Rapidly Integrated Transformation Technique), created by Meryl Hershey Beck and Robin Trainor Masci, two therapists who specialize in trauma and 12 Step Recovery. Over the years, these two women observed that their clients, due to the nature of the trauma they'd experienced in their lives, needed more spiritual support in releasing residual shock and grief. They masterfully wove the energy of Higher Power into the wording of RITT and the formula is impeccably effective in dissolving long-standing emotional misery.

RITT, similar to other energy tapping techniques, uses the acupuncture points to neutralize the charge of a painful issue. What gives RITT its sophistication is that this technique releases the trauma at its "deepest roots" AND replaces it with the somatic realization of emotional congruence. The beauty of RITT is that you don't have to identify an exact feeling. You don't have to recall a specific memory or situation. You don't even have to know what the precise difficulty is. If you're just feeling generally angry, or generally sad, or generally anxious and don't even know why, you can use RITT to get to the roots of the feeling and transform it.

Your painful False Identities need to be released and transformed. RITT not only will lead you to the dissolution of the old identity, it will help you begin to recognize the deeper truth of who you are. From there you can give words to your real and true, most noble and powerful, inherently perfect identity — the pure potential that you are.

So to begin, select the most prominent False Identity causing you the most pain. The one that, when you recognize it or admit it, hurts you right in your very heart or gut. The one that can bring you to tears, dejection, or defeat. Now turn to Appendix B. Slowly and gently guide yourself through the steps of RITT outlined for you. Take your time. Feel the feelings so you can tell when they subside. Feel the effects of a higher power.

Would you like to take it a little further?

Ms. Trainor Masci suggests another strategy. After you identify a False Identity and clear the charge, then "future pace" it and tap through RITT. Think of all the ways this identity might show up in your world in the future. Imagine a situation and clear any discomfort. Then place the "new" identity — the deeper truth of who you are, the *you* with pure potential — in that situation.

Keep imagining the different situations involving the False Identity…clear…future pace…substitute the True Identity.

Really take the time to do this. Your thinking, your beliefs, and your life will change.

CHAPTER 11

The Map of Consciousness

AS WE CLEAR OUR negative thoughts and beliefs and identities, a very clear elevation of our personal power opens up for us.

Dr. David Hawkins, M.D., PhD., in his book ***Power vs. Force,*** has literally mapped out this elevation in something he has coined as the "Map of Consciousness." One of the goals of his study was to "generate a practical map of the energy fields of consciousness…" And that he did. We now have a chart of the power of the energies of differing emotions, beginning with the lowest and leveling up to the highest.

Our emotions are clear indicators of our thoughts. That alone is powerful. But our emotions also are acknowledged as the voice of our soul. According to Gregg Braden, author of several science/spirituality books, human emotion is the language of what he terms the Divine Matrix — " a primal web of energy that connects your bodies, the world, and everything in the universe."

Dr. Hawkins' Map of Consciousness calculates the "power ranges" of the energy fields of specific emotions. These calibrations, ranging from 20 to 1000, are logarithmic (step by step progressions) and Dr. Hawkins reminds us that this is very different from mathematical increases.

He tells us "Thus, the level of 300 in not twice the amplitude of 150; it is 10 to the 300th power... An increase of even a few points represents a major advance in power; the rate of increase in power as we move up the scale is enormous."

Just being alive would be a shade above of 0.

At the bottom of the Map of Consciousness is SHAME, an energy field which calibrates at 20, which Dr. Hawkins states is "perilously proximate to death." Shame, according to Sigmund Freud, an Austrian neuropsychologist who lived from 1856 until 1939, is a basic cause of neuroses in a person. It's a consequence of low self-esteem and makes a person vulnerable to all kinds of emotional, psychological and physical illness. Believe it or not, some rigid and intolerant people who seem driven in their actions actually are shame-based. They also might tend to be shy and withdrawn, introverted as well as perfectionistic.

It goes up from there.

The next energy level of consciousness is GUILT, which registers at 30.

In Dr. Hawkins' words: Guilt "manifests itself in a variety of expressions, such as remorse, self-recrimination, masochism, and the whole gamut of symptoms of victim-hood. Unconscious guilt results in psychosomatic disease, accident-proneness, and suicidal behaviors." Guilt is commonly used to manipulate, control, dominate or punish.

The next level is APATHY, which calibrates at 50.

It manifests as helplessness and hopelessness and the ensuing inertia such a person feels in those states. Apathy is seen in the attitudes of poverty and despair.

GRIEF, the energy level of 75

The obvious manifestation of grief is mourning and bereavement. Grief is also about remorse over the past and not being able to recover what had been lost, as in the loss of a loved one. Grief is the level of deep sadness, irreparable loss and dependency. Yet it is an emotional energy above Apathy because Grief "feels." Apathy does not.

FEAR, 100, the next level up

Fear has a lot more range of energy than Grief. It is an emotion of worry and is very common in societies. It can grow into trepidation, obsession or paranoia and has a tendency to be contagious among people.

DESIRE, energy level of 125

Desire is a motivational energy and thus higher than Fear. However, Desire can spiral downward into an attitude of greed and even become an addiction. Desire can be an insatiable need to be fulfilled, or an inspiration to achieve higher levels of awareness.

ANGER, an even higher level of energy, registering at 150

Anger is most often expressed in relationships as resentment, a subtle form. Or anger can be violent. As Dr. Hawkins cites, "Anger as a lifestyle is exemplified by irritable, explosive people who are oversensitive to slights and become 'injustice collectors,' quarrelsome, belligerent, or litigious."

PRIDE, level 175

"Pride, which calibrates at 175, has enough energy to run the United States Marine Corps."

Pride is a big jump in energy because it looks and feels positive and good. Yet it's dependent upon unpredictable and subjective conditions — a very vulnerable position to be in. Pride also can be the basis of arrogance, which can be a divisive influence in societies.

The level of 200 is called the "CRITICAL LINE" on the chart because it's the level where *power* first appears. It is the first level that distinguishes between the negative and positive influences of the energy ranges on the map of consciousness. Below the level of 200, all test subjects went "weak." Above the critical line, Dr. Hawkins reports that, "Everyone goes strong in response to the life-supportive fields above 200."

COURAGE, the energy level of consciousness calibrating at 200

This is the level of empowerment, where one sees life as exciting and stimulating and enjoys challenges. Before this level people tend to view life as hopeless, sad or scary.

NEUTRALITY, the energy/consciousness level of 250

The reason this registers higher than even Courage is that Neutrality does not create opposition or division. The levels below this do create polarization. Neutrality is nonjudgmental and not attached to any desired outcomes.

Those who live in neutrality have a sense of well-being and generate a feeling of safety for others.

WILLINGNESS, the energy level of 310

There is rapid growth in this range because there is no longer resistance to life. Those at this level are friendly and helpful, and willing to process and resolve their inner issues.

ACCEPTANCE, the level of 350

This is a level of major transformation, where one takes responsibility for oneself as the source and creator of their experiences. This is the beginning of taking back one's power.

REASON, the level of 400

This is the level of knowledge and education, either scientific or medical. Many of the great figures in history are from this field. Although Reason calibrates so high, it can be an enormous block to higher levels of consciousness. It has been generally uncommon to rise above this level in society.

LOVE, the level of 500

This is too good not to quote most of it. So here goes.

"Love as depicted in the mass media is not what this level is about. What the world generally refers to as *love* is an intense emotional condition, combining physical attraction, possessiveness, control, addiction, eroticism, and novelty. It's usually fragile and fluctuating, waxing and waning with varying conditions. When frustrated, this emotion often reveals an underlying anger and dependency that it had masked. That love can turn into hate is a common perception, but here, an addictive sentimentality is likely what's being spoken about, rather than Love; there probably never was actual love in such a relationship, for Hate stems from Pride, not Love.

The 500 level is characterized by the development of a Love that is unconditional, unchanging, and permanent. It doesn't fluctuate — its source isn't dependent on external factors. Loving is a state of being. It's a forgiving, nurturing, and supportive way of relating to the world. Love isn't intellectual and doesn't proceed from the mind; Love emanates from the heart. It has the capacity to lift others and accomplish great feats because of its purity of motive."

"Love takes no position, and thus is global, rising above separation. It's then possible to be 'one with another,' for there are no longer any barriers. Love is, therefore, inclusive and expands the sense of self progressively. Love focuses on the goodness in life in all its expressions and augments that which is positive — it dissolves negativity by non-contextualizing it, rather than by attacking it."

"This is the level of true happiness, but although the world is fascinated with the subject of Love, and all viable religions calibrate at 500 or over, it's interesting to note that only 0.4 percent of the world's population ever reaches this level of evolution of consciousness."

*AS TO THIS LAST SENTENCE, I SAY **"NOT ANY MORE!"** NOT AFTER YOU READ THIS BOOK, AND DO YOUR INTERIOR WORK.*

JOY, the energy level of 540

Joy is the persistence of a positive attitude that arises from unconditional love. This is the level of the saints and spiritual healers. At this level a person sees the perfection of love and divinity in everything. A "Presence," a higher power, is felt by the person. This is the level of compassion and the dedication of one's consciousness for the benefit of all of life.

PEACE, the level of 600

This is a level of bliss and God-consciousness. At this level a person is inclined to move away from the influence of the world and observe that "everything is connected to everything else by a Presence whose power is infinite, exquisitely gentle, yet rock solid."

ENLIGHTENMENT, the levels of 700–1000

This is the level of the Spiritual Masters. It is the level of inspiration and an identification with Divine Consciousness. The highest calibration of divine grace at 1000 is the level of power of the "Great Avatars…. Lord Krishna, Lord Buddha, and Lord Jesus Christ."

I present this Map of Consciousness to you to illustrate that your emotions have vibrational qualities possessing what Dr. Hawkins termed "ranges of power." If you were to call to mind an example of how each emotion presented itself in your life, and felt its impact even right now in the present moment, you would feel the difference of each level of emotion.

Recall an instance when something caused you to feel shame in your life. How did it feel to experience shame? Take your time and feel the emotion. Recall an occasion when you were afraid. How did it feel to experience fear? Again feel the experience of this emotion and notice how it is different from shame. Bring to mind a memory of Joy. No need to give words to the feelings. Simply be aware of them. Even in your memory they have their own "words."

Do a kindness to yourself and clear the traumas of the lower levels as you climb the Map of Consciousness. Get a very real sense of what quality of power each emotion contains. Clear the triggers you have of shame, guilt, apathy, grief, fear, addictive desire, and anger or resentment. Bring up the feelings you have about these emotions, one at a time. Focus on one specific emotion and clear it.

Let's take a brief look at shame. If you choose to use EFT, go as far back in your memory as you can to recall the earliest time you experienced shame. Ask yourself what age you were. Can you go back any further than that? You want to get to your earliest memory of the "original wound." No need to get all hung up on if the memory was actually the earliest or not, because the original event probably happened way before you were even conscious of it. Just remember the first awareness you have of experiencing shame. Hold that event in your mind, and all the feelings you have about what happened, and the thoughts you think about whomever. Use EFT to give words to what you're experiencing. Do the number of rounds you need to do in order to reduce the discomfort you feel.

Or, if shame is such a pervasive obstruction in your life you cannot pull up a specific memory right now, use RITT.

At your own pace and in your own time, continue to clear the triggers you have in each level of emotion. You may even want to write down memories or feelings as they come up so that you don't forget to clear them later. Fear, grief, and anger will surely emerge as you deal with shame. And, as you know, they're not going to go anywhere. Their energies will stay put in your body and wait for you to release them.

Tender Heart's levels of emotion rose, with the cleaning of the rocks and boulders and hoodoos. Our levels rise with the clearing of our negative thoughts and beliefs and identities. As you free yourself from their heaviness and density you'll create the ability to reside in the higher ranges of power.

Tender Heart's path, as she climbs the Map of Consciousness, is the universal story of evolution. It is the ascension in consciousness that every human being is here on earth to participate in. At first the climb is difficult and then, at a certain point, it becomes easy and then — a way of life.

CHAPTER 12

Crossing the Threshold:
The Hundredth Monkey

A MYSTIC FROM THE 16th century, St. Teresa of Avila, describes the very same path, beginning as a challenge and then growing in ease towards being a way of life. She describes this as the "journey of the soul" in her writings known as ***The Interior Castle.*** And it looks something like this.

Imagine a crystal, the shape of a castle, with 7 chambers, which are called "mansions" spiraling deeper and deeper in towards the center. St. Teresa calls these levels mansions because each is an elaborate labyrinth of hallways and huge rooms with cabinets and closets and things (like furniture) to bump into; things to trip over (like rugs, thresholds, small footstools, etc.); things that keep us lingering too long (like beautiful art pieces, paintings, glittery chandeliers…); and all kinds of places to get lost in. All these things represent the obstacles and distractions in our soul's journey.

From the center of the castle a brilliant light emanates, illuminating the entire structure. The crystal castle rests on a piece of black velvet, much like the fabric jewelers use to display the brilliant facets of gems that they are showing to clients. The velvet represents the blackness in which live, what St. Teresa called, the "vermin and pestilence" — her words for our compulsions and addictions.

The journey begins with the soul's choice to leave the darkness and travel towards the light. As the soul enters the castle and proceeds through the first 4 mansions the compulsions and addictions keep reaching for it, trying to grab it back outside into the blackness. The danger is still very high for the soul to be clutched back into the darkness. And it must be aware and diligent about the paths it chooses to navigate through each room and hallway of each chamber. It's a difficult journey in the beginning to travel from one level to the next, not only because of the obstacles and distractions and the unknown territory, but also because of the vermin and pestilence.

By the 5th chamber, it's far more difficult for the "venomous creatures" to grab the soul, and so it proceeds safely with much more ease into the next mansion, following the light ahead which is getting brighter with each level. The journey continues to get easier and easier because the soul becomes aware of being led. By the 6th chamber, the energy shifts. The soul is now feeling absolutely compelled to get to the source of the beautiful light and runs faster towards it with joy and great anticipation. The light becomes more and more brilliant and by the time the soul gets to the 7th chamber it is fully alive with eagerness as it races towards the light. And then the soul finds itself standing before the innermost chamber of the castle.

As the soul enters into the innermost chamber, it finds itself in the presence of the source of the illumination. The brilliant light is the King of the castle who has been waiting for the soul to arrive. And, in that final interior chamber the soul is at last in complete bliss as it unites with the King in ecstatic, sacred marriage. In that union they are One; they are Oneness.

The 5th chamber is quite a turning point for the soul, for it reaches what is called "critical mass" — the threshold at which enough effort and action is gathered that a fundamental change occurs and the interior journey becomes easier.

Humanity's journey in consciousness, a well, contains within it thresholds of critical mass. With each teaching of the Great Avatars and ascended Masters we, along the eons of time, have been given the precepts of higher consciousness. Fortunately, the Great Religions of the world have preserved these precepts for us. Jesus the Christ, the Buddha, Lord Krishna, mentioned by Dr. Hawkins, shared the knowledge of the "critical line" (the level of consciousness that distinguishes between the negative and positive influences of the energy ranges of power on the Map of Consciousness). From each of these Masters and other great spiritual teachers, momentum has gathered into critical mass that has reached into our current time ushering us into higher consciousness.

And what is "critical mass"? It can be demonstrated in the story of the "hundredth monkey effect." As the report goes, a group of Japanese scientists were observing the behavior of monkeys on the island of Koshima in 1952. And by the way, these are NOT monkeys gone wild on sugar and booze.

Some of the older monkeys began to wash the sweet potatoes they dug up before they would eat them. The younger monkeys observed their actions and gradually began to imitate the new behavior and then kept repeating it. When enough monkeys (critical mass) on that island adopted the new behavior, some way — some how, the knowledge of that behavior jumped over to the next island. And when enough monkeys on that next island implemented the behavior, it transferred to the next island. And on and on.

And this is how it goes in the human community, too.

Who knows? Maybe Bella Divina was the hundredth monkey for Tender Heart.

Because of her willingness to listen to the wisdom of Bella Divina and release her pain, Tender Heart gathered enough critical mass in the process to cross the threshold into the greater consciousness of love. From there her journey on the Path of Love was easier and more fulfilling.

Maybe Tender Heart is our hundredth monkey.

In terms of consciousness, humanity is reaching critical mass. More and more people are "getting there." What the sages and saints and enlightened Masters have been saying to us throughout the millennia — the teachings that got them ostracized or crucified or condemned as enemies of the state, the wisdom that got them banished or punished or left penniless because they spoke a truth that others couldn't grasp — are becoming understandable to the masses now. And furthermore, these things are becoming accepted in the society of man due to the discoveries of science. Humanity is finally able to reach, en mass, the heights of ascended wisdom that only the mystics experienced in days gone by.

If humanity so chooses.

It begins with choice. Choosing to take the journey of enlightenment or "lighten-up-ment" as it's affectionately known. Choosing to clean up our own internal world as Tender Heart chose. Choosing to share the wisdom and behaviors we learn.

Choosing to stay on the journey.

When we arrive at the threshold of our emotional journey's critical mass, consciousness gets easier. As more and more of us implement the behavior of washing our grimy false identities away, it all gets easier for humanity. Just ask the hundredth monkey.

CHAPTER 13

The Law of Pure Desire

THE LAW OF PURE DESIRE states that when the intention behind your desire is pure — not motivated by fear or desperation — a beneficial outcome is certain.

The energetics behind this concept are:

Fear and desperation *resonate* (remember that Law?) as resistant, negative frequencies. The inclusion of them in an intention unmistakably indicates some sort of focus on them, which destroys the purity and strength of the intention.

Furthermore, inclusion of these energies in an intention will attract more of their frequencies into your field. The precision of the intention requires that your motivation is *only that which you desire.*

Any motives of seeking to eliminate something you don't want, or of escaping a problem you don't want to have, will also negate the purity or the precision of the intention. Any thoughts of acquiring something, to fill a need you think you have, will destroy its precision as well.

Declare your desire not from the energy that resides in your head, aka 'thinking,' but rather from the energy that resides in the center of your body. Some would call it the heart space; some might name it the soul. This deep desire — that you really mean it when you speak it — wells up from the very core of you. Really feel the innermost center where your desire is emanating from. And speak from there.

Speak out loud. This puts your desire into the airwaves. It puts it "out there." It is supremely powerful to release desire from the recesses of your physical structure, for then it's set into motion. The Law of Pure Desire also necessitates giving up any attachment or expectation as to the wanted outcome. You simply state your desire without hoping or expecting. Simply state firmly to the universe or God or higher power, that this is your very clear desire.

End of story.

Period.

And then go about your way and detach from any expectation or anticipation. Your conscious mind needs to let go of obsessing, whining, and pining. First of all, because those are a gross (dense, low vibrating) energy to be around and will repulse higher energies. Secondly, you will attract the same quality of energy you're putting out. And finally, because these energies destroy the purity and precision of the intention. Let go of constantly thinking about getting what you want. (Easier said than done, I know.)

Your subconscious mind then will begin to organize around your desire. In mysterious, sometimes convoluted, sometimes wild and crazy ways, seemingly unrelated events will line up to fulfill that desire. And a wonderful outcome will manifest in ways that will surprise and delight you.

Just relax about it all and enjoy the ride.

CHAPTER 14

The Field of Love

TENDER HEART, through her travels in consciousness on the Path of Love, experienced a shift in her way of *being*. She entered into a greater understanding of the "morphogenic field" of Love. She had toyed with its peripheries throughout her life, but she did not fully resonate with it and she did not commit to it.

The first segment of her journey was spent struggling on the path of human behaviors, and feeling their emotional consequences. Essentially, she was living on the surface. Just walking the walk of rocks and boulders and hoodoos; negative thoughts and false beliefs. But then she stopped and took the time to dislodge and disengage from her judgments and negative beliefs. The next segment then led her to greater insight and understanding, and surprisingly different developments.

What is this thing called the "morphogenic field of Love"? Simply put, a morphogenic field is an energy consisting of its own specific frequencies and influences.

We are encompassed by and permeated by an intelligence or field called "Universal energy," also spoken of as "Mind" — with a capital "M" — (small "m" refers to the human mind.) And in terms of human existence, this intelligence, greater than we — which is around us and within us — is inextricably connected to human emotion.

When we are in alignment with the Universal energy of Love we actually experience the fullness and satiation, the expansion and bliss, of its field of energy. We are immersed in the higher ranges of power that Dr. Hawkins describes in the Map of Consciousness. When we are not in alignment with the energy of Love, we're not able to access its field, nor its emotional properties; nor are we able to extend its harmonic sine waves (Chapter 2) beyond ourselves.

It all works something like this:

We choose to live our lives a certain way. Each and every day, sometimes minute-by-minute, we determine the way we will conduct our lives and decide how we will behave. We've already seen how we've chosen to think our thoughts and believe our beliefs; and how to neutralize those that do not serve the highest expression of our lives.

Whatever it is that we choose — that we align with — triggers a process within us. Something begins to change, to evolve, and to transform within the very cells of our body energetically. This change inside our body actually affects our outside physical world and begins to interact with the powerful force of creation. We, in essence, create the operational workings of our lives; therefore, we are the cause of the effects that ensue. Our actions of one sort (say of "compassion") will elicit a different response than actions of another sort (say of "contempt".)

The degree to which we desire, and believe, and Be the energy of Love is the experience we will have in (and of) the world.

CHAPTER 15

The Phantom Effect of Our Relationships

UNDOUBTEDLY, THERE IS A connection at the most quantum, and as yet invisible, level between us, and the space we inhabit. Clearly, scientific evidence points to something most of us feel, but cannot figure out a way to verbalize. We are indeed directly linked with our fellow man and the world around us. Recent scientific breakthroughs powered by rapidly advancing technology are now proving what our souls have known for eons.

We live in a "quantum hologram" meaning that matter emits, receives, and interacts with other matter at a quantum — "the smallest unit of energy" — level. (Dr. Walter Schempp) Similarly, the subtle energies of human emotion are also emitted and received and interacted with physically, face-to-face, cell-to-cell, and at the quantum level.

I'd like to paraphrase some research concerning the subtle energy phenomenon known as the "DNA phantom effect." Here's the nutshell version of the findings of Dr. Vladimir Poponin and Dr. Peter Gariaev.

They placed specimens of human DNA into what are known as scattering chambers, which had originally contained only light particles. The light particles (photons), which were hanging around randomly, did something totally unexpected when the DNA was placed into the tube with them — they organized themselves into orderly patterns. The radiation (light particles), coupled with the DNA's field, created new "physical substructures."

The bigger surprise happened when the DNA was removed. The photons, through some invisible force, *remained* in the newly formed substructures as if the living material were still present, sometimes for weeks. This phenomenon is called the "DNA phantom effect," and is part of the larger category of "electromagnetic phantom effect." I share this with you in order to illustrate a point.

Something similar happens in the world of the subtle energies of our *emotions*, which are extraordinary conduits of energy and communication. Let's look at it this way: Here we are in our very own "scattering chamber" of being-ness, with the subtle energies of our emotions hanging around randomly, until we experience the influence of another person, either in physical form or energetic form, or even in our thoughts about such person. The combination of their influence in our "chamber" of emotions forms a new substructure of frequency. This would be called a "relationship." Yep. At that point we are in relationship with that person. Subtly, sub-atomically, emotionally, and physically.

Think of a person you know right now. Any person. The first one who pops in your mind. Just check your "innards" to see what kind of relationship you're in at the moment with that person. Do you feel warm and fuzzy or do you feel twisted in knots? Do you feel a lot of love or do you feel anger? Do you feel neutral and curious, or do you feel superior and judgmental? Whatever relationship you're in with that person in your thoughts is important because chances are it will play out in similar fashion in the external world at some point. Ultimately the relationship we have with a person at a quantum level, in our thoughts and emotions, will show up in physical reality through our words and actions.

The good news in all of this is that we are in charge of how it will go. Based on our level of consciousness, we determine the quality of the new substructure that is formed. Our relationships can be easy or difficult, peaceful or tumultuous, healing or devastating.

Remember the galactic beings from Chapter 7? The ones 30,000 miles above, who can only witness the goings-on of humans? To them we'd just be bunches of DNA intermingling and intertwining and combining. What they would see in the new substructures we create with others would be newly formed patterns of: unity or separation, growth or stagnation, destruction or evolution.

Our emotions are the messengers of the level of consciousness (Dr. David Hawkins' Map) at which we resonate. They are the language through which our heart energy expresses. And we transmit the subtle energies of our emotions in the substructures of our relationships.

We humans, who come into this world as pure potentiality, possess the abilities of rational thought and raw emotion. And in ways we don't even understand yet, we actually emit our thoughts and emotions.

In conclusion:

The seriously number one emotion that motivates a human being's life is love — in all its assorted forms — the sharing and caring of it (or not)…. the giving and receiving of it (or not).

The template of love's morphogenic field is one of expansion and creation. Its influencing principles are those of harmony, appreciation, honesty, integrity, respect and even reverence. These, and so many other aspects of love, become manifest in our physical world when we bring them in and try them on, and emit them.

Thus, the relationships that are born are nurtured and matured; **and leave legacies.**

This is the story of the human journey. Our journey. The journey of our soul. And the journey of our heart.

Tender Heart found herself in the Force and Field of Love because she sought to resonate with love. It is here that she was invited to create a life that she couldn't have manifested before.

Now she is in the conscious knowing of love's morphogenic field, because she lives **in** and **as** love.

And as she learns to envision and create and magnetize to herself the future she desires and **intends,** she'll find herself smack dab in the middle of the next Chapters of Her Journey.

Just like us.

Emotional Freedom Technique

BEGIN BY CALLING TO MIND the original wound. On a scale of zero to 10, with 10 being the worst pain ever and zero being no pain at all, rate the severity of feelings when you would recall an item on your list or the feelings around the item.

Start with what is called the Setup. It consists of 3 statements, generally similar.

While saying the Setup statement (3 times) simply tap, with the four fingertips of one hand, on the karate chop area of the other hand. It doesn't matter which hand does what.

"Even though _________________, I TOTALLY AND COMPLETELY ACCEPT MYSELF."

"Even though _________________________, I DEEPLY AND COMPLETELY ACCEPT MYSELF."

"Even though _________________________, I TOTALLY LOVE AND ACCEPT MYSELF."

OR

You can change the words around.

"Even though _________________________, I TOTALLY AND COMPLETELY LOVE MYSELF."

"Even though _________________________, I COMPLETELY LOVE AND ACCEPT MYSELF."

Even if you can't believe the part "I totally and completely accept, or love, myself," even if you choke on the words just say them, because it's not about the words anyway. There is a part of you that may not want to release the negative emotions or feelings. The Setup is about giving the subconscious mind (where the transforming takes place) time to kick into gear. And as Gary Craig says "While you're waiting, you might as well say something nice to yourself." An extra, added bonus is that over time you actually start to believe the words and begin to accept and even love yourself.

Let's do a practice round.

EVEN THOUGH MEN (OR WOMEN) ABANDON ME OVER AND OVER AGAIN, I TOTALLY AND COMPLETELY ACCEPT MYSELF.

You can repeat this exact statement 2 more times, or say other statements. Such as:

Even though men don't really care about me and always leave me, I deeply and completely accept myself.

Even though I would never trust a man to stay in my life, I completely and totally accept myself.

Just say what is true for you. Three statements only.

After the Setup, you will begin to tap very lightly (with 2 or 3 fingertips of each hand) and pretty fast, on meridian/acupressure points in a certain sequence as you speak out loud. Tapping lightly is quite a good thing to do, since you probably don't want to give yourself a headache or leave little red spots on your body. Most novices tend to tap harder than need be, because they feel awkward or just want to make sure it "takes." No need.

Let's keep going with our example, referring to the tapping points diagram on the following page:

Tap on the Crown, the top of the head where the strings would attach if you were a puppet. This is where you get to let all the emotions start pouring out in your words.

Tap with your fingertips and keep tapping 5 to 7 times or until you are finished with your sentence or phrase. You will repeat this procedure for each acupressure point.

I cannot believe that __________ treated me that way.

(You can name the person, call them a jerk or worse… these tapping points are where you get to speak your unpretty thoughts and feel the emotions of your pain)

Move down to the area between the eyebrows. It's known, also, as the "third eye."

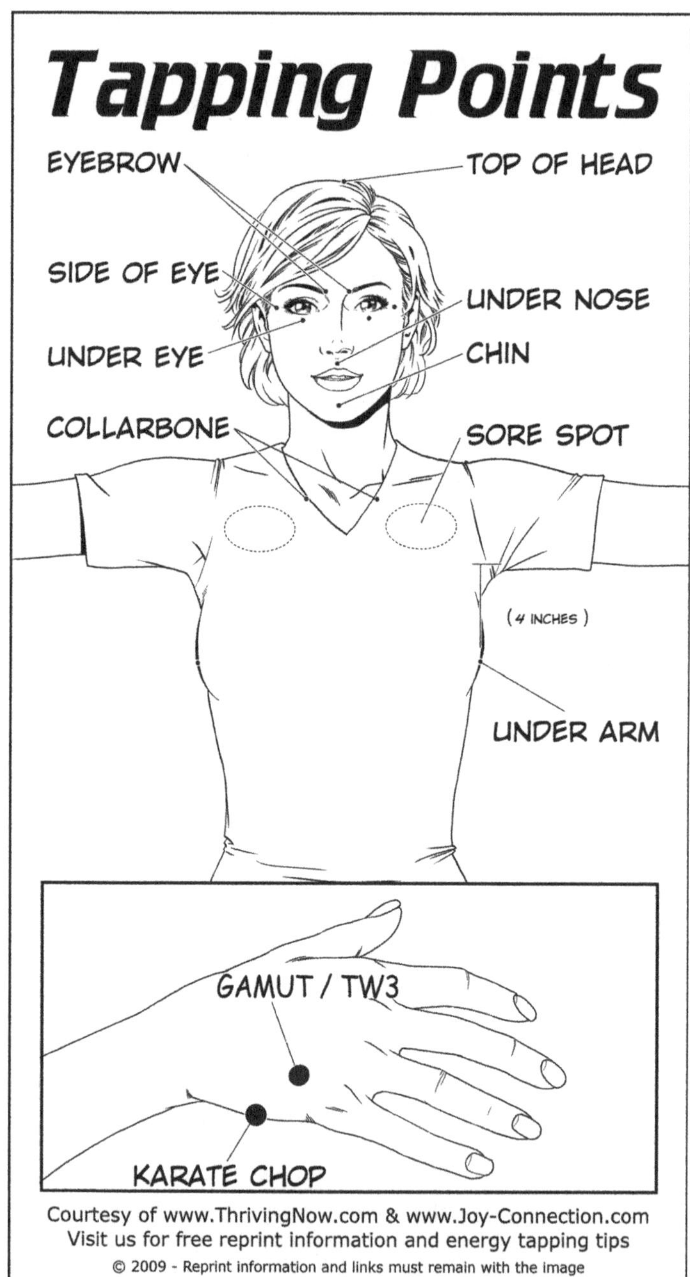

Tapping Points
EYEBROW
TOP OF HEAD
SIDE OF EYE
UNDER NOSE
UNDER EYE
CHIN
COLLARBONE
SORE SPOT
(4 INCHES)
UNDER ARM
GAMUT / TW3
KARATE CHOP
Courtesy of www.ThrivingNow.com & www.Joy-Connection.com
Visit us for free reprint information and energy tapping tips
© 2009 - Reprint information and links must remain with the image

Tap and keep tapping until you've finished your sentence or phrase.

I WAS SO SCARED WHEN HE/SHE HIT ME... YELLED AT ME... LEFT ME...WHATEVER IS TRUE FOR YOU.

Move to the inside edge of the eyebrows, where the brow meets the skin.

You can tap the inside edge of each brow in unison or alternately. You can tap with one hand back and forth or with both hands staying directly over each inside edge of each eyebrow.

I MUST MEAN NOTHING TO HIM/HER.

Move to the side of both eyes, on the bony socket near the temples.

Tap.

HOW COULD HE/SHE DO THAT TO ME KNOWING HOW MUCH I CARED ABOUT HIM/HER? I HATE HIM/HER FOR LEAVING.

I know that sounds a little strong. We're just trying to get to the honest emotion that you would feel.

Move to under the eyes on the bony socket directly centered under the iris of the eye. Be sure to tap on the bone and not on the delicate skin in the under eye area.

WHAT IF I NEVER SEE HIM/HER AGAIN? WHAT IF NO ONE WILL EVER LOVE ME?

Move to above the upper lip, where the indented area is under the nose.

Tap.

I'M SO SCARED. I'M SO AFRAID OF BEING ALONE.

Move to under the bottom lip, in the indented ridge, towards the ball of the chin.

Tap.

HOW WILL I SURVIVE WITHOUT LOVE? I DON'T THINK I CAN.

Move to the collarbone area. This place is a little tricky so you'll have to feel around for the precise spots.

First feel into the notch of your throat just under the Adam's apple. The bone bordering the lowest area of the soft flesh feels U Shaped, almost V Shaped. The collarbone, on both sides, extends out from that notched area. Follow the collarbone in both directions with your fingertips, going outward laterally about an inch or so until it feels like the bone kind of dips, or bows in. These are the points you will tap. Beginners tend to drift off to the far ends of the collarbone towards the shoulders, so the effort to find these points and then be mindful of them is well worth the time taken to do so. No need to drive yourself crazy trying to decide if you're in the right place. With the tapping of your two or three fingers in both those near-the-notch areas you are guaranteed effectiveness.

So now tap.

"THERE MUST BE SOMETHING VERY WRONG ABOUT ME. NO ONE WANTS ME. I'M SO BAD!"

Move to the under arm area. To find these points, first fully extend your arms out ward with your palms facing down. Keep your upper arms from the shoulders to the elbows straight out and then from the elbow joint simply drop the lower part of your arms straight down towards the floor. It would look like the arms of the perfect T formation you had been holding broke at a 90-degree angle in the middle. Then from that 90-degree angle keep bringing your forearms towards the sides of your body. Where your fingertips touch the sides is where the points are.

For women, this is an easy location to find. It is the bra area at the sides of the body.

Tap.

"WHAT WILL I DO? IF I'M THIS BAD NOBODY COULD EVER WANT ME."

Move to what is called the Liver points. Don't worry. You don't need to know which side your liver is on because these points are not there. They are located at the first rib underneath the breast. Again, women luck out finding these. Go down to the first ribs underneath the underwire of the bra. The points are there and centered underneath each nipple. The points are there as well for men; they just don't have the landmark advantage women have. But with the 2 or 3 or even 4 fingertip span, success is guaranteed.

Begin to tap.

"I AM NO GOOD. I DON'T DESERVE TO HAVE ANYONE LOVE ME. I'M SCUM."

This is the end of what is called a "round."

At this point you will take a break. ***Simply breathe in deeply and exhale slowly and fully.***

Maybe just take another breath for good measure. Notice how you feel. Don't be surprised that even though you left off at calling yourself scum you may feel peaceful and actually pretty good. What happened is that you released the honest to goodness feelings you'd been holding in for ages — ones you probably didn't even know you'd been harboring.

On a scale of zero to 10, with 10 being the worst you could feel and zero being no pain at all, rate your discomfort. If the "charge" (the "pain") went down that is great. If the charge went up as it sometimes might do, that is okay as well. It just means a little more neutralizing needs to take place. The goal is to get to zero if possible.

Here's the outline of EFT:

Bring a memory to mind
Rate your discomfort on a scale of 1–10
3 Set-up statements: " Even though…"
Tap the points while speaking
    Crown
    Inside of eyebrows
    Outside of eyes
    Underneath the eyes
    Above the lips
    Below the lips
    Collarbone notches
    Under the armpits
    Liver points
Take a deep breath to clear out the energy
Rate how you now feel
Continue, if need be

Your options for taking the remaining charge down are numerous. You might do another round. You might change it up and do a variation of EFT called "Choices."

"Choices" consists of 3 rounds. As always, rate your discomfort on a scale of 0–10 and then begin. In the first round you would speak all the negative emotions that you recall about the issue you're tapping on. In the second round, you'd speak all the positive things that you can think of about the issue — like how you've grown because of it, or the good things in your life because of it, things like that. In the third round you would alternate negative and positive statements. And as usual, at the end of the 3 rounds you'd take a deep breath and exhale slowly. Then rate your discomfort again. If not to zero, then repeat another 3 rounds. Rate again.

For stubborn issues there is EFT plus the 9 Gamut Sequence. Or you could simply switch to another energy technique. You can learn these options and then put them together as you sense the need for them.

The 9 Gamut Procedure is:

Tap on your issue using EFT, and at the end of it tap on the karate chop point (on fleshy outside edge of hand, between base of little finger and wrist) of one hand with 3 or 4 fingers of the other hand. Then, without moving your head, start to tap on the back of the same hand between the little finger and the ring finger, half an inch towards your wrist. You can feel the "v" of the little finger and the ring finger bones come together. There is a slight depression at this point. This is the Gamut Point, aka the "Brain Balancer." You will keep tapping during the next 9 actions.

Eyes Closed

Eyes Open

Eyes look hard down on the floor, to your right

Eyes look hard down on the floor, to your left

> Roll your eyes in a complete circle, going left or right — it doesn't matter
>
> Roll eyes in the other direction
>
> Hum (do not sing) 5 seconds of a song —
>
> Suggestion: the "do-re-mi" scale or "Happy Birthday"
>
> Count to 5: 1 – 2 – 3 – 4 – 5
>
> Hum (don't sing) the scale or song again

Rate your discomfort again. If you still have some discomfort, then go back the crown and tap the EFT sequence again. The EFT — 9 Gamut — EFT procedure constitutes a "set." Several sets might be needed to eliminate the discomfort.

And again, the 9 Gamut Procedure is rarely used — only in very stubborn cases.

The more specific you can be with whatever your issue is, the better the results.

Because this may be new to you, and because I took some time to explain some things, these rounds and sets may have seemed interminable. There is a learning curve to be sure but once EFT is learned and becomes part of your skills toolkit, you will find that a round literally only takes 5 minutes; 10 if you want to speak paragraphs instead of short sentences.

Rapidly Integrated Transformation Technique

Meryl Hershey Beck and Robin Trainor Masci, both enlightened, innovative therapists having over 30 years of experience with trauma and addiction recovery, have given RITT to the world.

This version, in the attempt to keep it consistent with the contents, is adapted from the original modality. Where the word IDENTITY appears here, the original version states CHALLENGE/ISSUE. In other contexts, these words could be supplanted by the words appropriate to the work at hand. For example, when clearing judgments the word JUDGMENT would be appropriate in each step. For resentment and trigger work the words RESENTMENT or TRIGGER would be apropos.

✱✱✱✱✱✱✱✱✱✱✱

Think of the issue you want to clear and notice the level of discomfort (from 0 = None to 10 = Intense).

Now imagine the metaphor of you being a tree. The branches represent your conscious mind and the roots are the subconscious mind. You will be clearing from the branches to the roots. As you lightly tap each point using 2 or 3 fingers (similar to EFT, so refer to Appendix A for details if you need to), think about the issue and read aloud the statements in quotations below.

1. **Karate Chop Point — outside edge of hand. Either hand is okay.**

    I RELEASE THIS IDENTITY/ISSUE TO HIGHER POWER (God/Spirit/Light/Love/ whatever name you want to give the power that is greater than yourself)

    TO TRANSFORM IT AND MY RELATIONSHIP TO IT, NEVER TO TAKE IT BACK OR PASSIVELY RECEIVE IT BACK.

2. **Heart Point — sore spot in the Pledge of Allegiance area, gently rub in a circle towards the shoulder. Repeat 3 times:**

    I LOVE AND ACCEPT MYSELF UNCONDITIONALLY EVEN THOUGH I HAVE THIS ISSUE.

3. **Crown (top of the head)**

    I BRING IN HIGHER POWER (GOD, SPIRIT, LIGHT ......) UP INTO ALL THE BRANCHES AND DOWN TO THE DEEPEST ROOTS OF THIS ISSUE, AND ASK FOR HEALING FOR THE HIGHEST GOOD.

4. **Eyebrow (either eyebrow, tap where the eyebrow starts, near the bridge of the nose)**

   I RELEASE ALL THE SADNESS IN ALL THE BRANCHES DOWN TO THE DEEPEST ROOTS OF THIS IDENTITY/ISSUE.

5. **Under eye (on the bone just below the eye, and centered under the eye)**

   I RELEASE ALL THE FEAR IN ALL THE BRANCHES DOWN TO THE DEEPEST ROOTS OF THIS IDENTITY/ISSUE.

6. **Under the nose and lower lip (using the sides of the thumb and index finger, tap both spots at once — side of index finger under the nose, and side of thumb under the lower lip at the indentation above the chin)**

   I RELEASE ALL THE SHAME AND EMBARRASSMENT IN ALL THE BRANCHES DOWN TO THE DEEPEST ROOTS AROUND THIS IDENTITY/ISSUE.

7. **Collarbone (tap two finger widths beneath inside of collarbones — close to the breastbone)**

   I RELEASE ALL THE HURT AND ALL THE GRIEF IN ALL THE BRANCHES DOWN TO THE DEEPEST ROOTS OF THIS IDENTITY/ISSUE.

8. **Under Arm (tender spot about 4 inches below the armpit, in line with the nipples)**

   I RELEASE ALL THE GUILT IN ALL THE BRANCHES DOWN TO THE DEEPEST ROOTS OF THIS IDENTITY/ISSUE.

9. **Third Eye (point between eyebrows)**
   I RELEASE ALL THE TRAUMA IN ALL THE BRANCHES DOWN TO THE DEEPEST ROOTS OF THIS IDENTITY/ISSUE.

10. **Inside wrist (tap where watchband would fasten, palm side of wrist)**
    I RELEASE ALL THE PAIN IN ALL THE BRANCHES DOWN TO THE DEEPEST ROOTS THIS IDENTITY/ISSUE.

11. **Little finger, side of the nail (tap on the side of the finger next to the ring finger)**
    I RELEASE ALL THE ANGER IN ALL THE BRANCHES DOWN TO THE DEEPEST ROOTS OF THIS IDENTITY/ISSUE.

12. **Side of the Index Finger (nearest the thumb)**
    Do at least 3 of the following:
    - I RELEASE ALL THE ENERGY INVESTED IN THIS ISSUE SO I CAN USE THAT ENERGY FOR MY OWN WELL-BEING.
    - I TOTALLY AND COMPLETELY FORGIVE MYSELF FOR FORGETTING THAT I AM DOING THE BEST I CAN.
    - I TOTALLY AND COMPLETELY FORGIVE MYSELF FOR ALLOWING THIS IDENTITY/ ISSUE TO DISTURB MY PEACE OF MIND.
    - I TOTALLY AND COMPLETELY FORGIVE MYSELF AND I INTEND TO FORGIVE EVERYONE ELSE INVOLVED.
    - I TOTALLY AND COMPLETELY FORGIVE MYSELF AND I ASK FOR THE WISDOM TO SEE THAT EVERYONE ELSE INVOLVED WAS ACTING FROM A PLACE OF UNMET NEEDS.

Breathe. Reassess your level of discomfort or level. If still greater than 0, repeat steps 1–12. When the intensity is at 0, continue to **Step 13** below.

13. **All spots in sequence from #4–#11:**

    I BRING IN HIGHER POWER (OR JOY OR LOVE OR PEACE…) TO REPLACE THE SADNESS IN ALL THE BRANCHES DOWN TO THE DEEPEST ROOTS OF THIS IDENTITY/ ISSUE.

    I BRING IN HIGHER POWER…TO REPLACE THE FEAR IN ALL THE BRANCHES DOWN TO THE DEEPEST ROOTS OF THIS IDENTITY/ISSUE.

    I BRING IN HIGHER POWER… TO REPLACE ALL THE SHAME AND ALL THE EMBARRASSMENT IN ALL THE BRANCHES DOWN TO THE DEEPEST ROOTS OF THIS IDENTITY/ISSUE.

    I BRING IN HIGHER POWER…TO REPLACE ALL THE HURT AND ALL THE GRIEF IN ALL THE BRANCHES DOWN TO THE DEEPEST ROOTS OF THIS IDENTITY/ISSUE.

    I BRING IN HIGHER POWER…TO REPLACE ALL THE GUILT IN ALL THE BRANCHES DOWN TO THE DEEPEST ROOTS OF THIS IDENTITY/ISSUE.

    I BRING IN HIGHER POWER…TO REPLACE ALL THE PAIN IN ALL THE BRANCHES DOWN TO THE DEEPEST ROOTS OF THIS IDENTITY/ ISSUE.

    I BRING IN HIGHER POWER…TO REPLACE ALL THE ANGER IN ALL THE BRANCHES DOWN TO THE DEEPEST ROOTS OF THIS IDENTITY/ISSUE.

I bring in higher power…to replace all the
trauma in all the branches down to the deepest roots of this identity/issue.

Take a deep breath.
It is complete.

Meryl Hershey Beck, M.A., M.Ed., LPCC
Personal Growth Expert, Counselor, and Author of
*Stop Eating Your Heart Out: The 21-Day Program
to Free Yourself from Emotional Eating*
www.stopeatingyourheartout.com

www.LearnRITT.com
Meryl Hershey Beck 520.661.7444
Robin Trainor Masci 520-449-3152

Definitions of Love

Just for further thought, I have included various "definitions" of love that I've discovered in my research.

As you will see, some of these are not hopeful or pleasant and can, in fact, be painful or offensive.

Here they are, simply put:

CONTEMPORARY DEFINITIONS

BANQUET — self-sacrificing love

LIMERENCE — an intense romantic attraction to someone with intense need to have it reciprocated.

LUDUS — love being used as a game; just for fun

MANIA — intense, possessive and obsessive love

NARCISSISTIC — only caring about oneself in a relationship, with little care for the partner's happiness

OBSESSIVE — takes limerence to a whole other level and borders on addiction to a person

PRAGMA — practical and rational love

PUPPY LOVE — cute and frivolous, spontaneous and shallowly based love

It can be argued that some of these particular interpretations of love are actually distortions and perhaps even abominations of love. You decide for yourself where you stand on this.

For sure they are a far cry from the Philosophical or Psychological definitions (below).

PHILOSOPHICAL DEFINITIONS

Ancient Greek philosophers categorized the following **five basic types** of love:

STORGE — Affectionate, accepting love that exists within a family unit.

PHILIA OR PHILIO — Love between friends. (Our eastern city of Philadelphia, the "city of brotherly love," was named to commemorate *philia*.)

EROS — Generally understood as the passion and sexual intimacy between lovers. (It 's derived from the Greek word 'erotas' which means "intimate love.")

Plato dissected *Eros* a little more by alluding to a love above plain ole *philio* and intense enough to be in the realm of eros, but not sexual. He endearingly named it *Platonic* love.

> *AGAPE* — The "highest love" — agape connotes a deep, abiding, unconditional love otherwise referred to as "divine love" or, in contemporary terms, "universal love."

PSYCHOLOGICAL APPROACH

According to psychologist, Elaine Hatfield PhD., co-author of several books and professor at the University of Hawaii, there are two types of love:

> *COMPASSIONATE LOVE* — comprised of mutual affection, respect, and trust.

> *PASSIONATE LOVE* — full of intense emotion, sexual chemistry, and elation. Be aware that ***mutual*** love and reciprocation are required, or there will be a deterioration into anxiety, depression or despair.

In the ideal world, Passionate Love would lead to and combine with enduring Compassionate Love. And this would be the same trifecta as Dr. Sternberg's Consummate Love.

Psychologist Robert Sternberg, PhD. developed the "Triangular Theory of Love," which points to three main components of love:

Passion,

Intimacy and

Commitment.

In his words, "Passion is the quickest to develop and the quickest to fade. Intimacy develops more slowly, and commitment more gradually still."

According to Dr. Sternberg these three elements combine in various ways to produce seven types of love:

LIKING —

Intimacy — Yes

Passion — No

Commitment — No

Characterized by a certain level of intimacy, but has no passion or commitment.

COMPANIONATE LOVE —

Intimacy — Yes

Commitment — Yes

Passion — No

This would be love for family members, or a long-term, formerly romantic relationship. We all could probably call to mind someone we know whose relationship tended toward this type of love after a while.

EMPTY LOVE —

Commitment — Yes

Intimacy — No

Passion — No

This would be seen in couples who live in the same dwelling but are leading very separate lives, or who stay together "for the kids."

FATUOUS LOVE —

Passion — Yes

Commitment — Yes

Intimacy — No

This would be the couple who have an instant connection and marry quickly without taking the time to get to know each other. And because they really don't have the intimacy needed, they struggle throughout their entire relationship, since they are committed to it, using their passion to make it work, or ***trying to make it work.***

INFATUATION —

Passion — Yes

Intimacy — No

Commitment — No

This is "love at first sight" and generally disappears without the grounding of commitment or the bonding of intimacy.

ROMANTIC LOVE —
Passion — Yes
Intimacy — Yes
Commitment — No
Emotional intensity, as it normalizes, usually fizzles out without the groundedness of commitment.

CONSUMMATE LOVE —
Intimacy — Yes
Passion — Yes
Commitment — Yes
The trifecta of intimacy, passion, AND commitment, each being equally as strong as the others.

This love weathers the storms of life. These "true-love-partners" are intimate, passionate, and committed to each other and to their relationship.

About the Author

BLESSED AS A WIFE OF 30 YEARS, mother of 7 children and educator, Janet St. Marie has been where her clients are. It was going through her own crucible of pain in an unexpected divorce that led her to seek out demonstrably effective methods for truly releasing and forgiving the past. Determined not to let circumstances dictate the future course of her emotional life, she didn't stop searching and exploring until she found the keys to genuinely re-opening herself to love.

Since emerging from her own deep well of hurt and disillusionment, Janet has dedicated herself to continuing her commitment to education, by teaching others the same techniques for creating personal empowerment and loving relationships.

She became certified as both an Energy Coach and a Calling in the One Coach in the process, incorporating proven formats for ensuring her clients have the greatest success in accessing these new skills.

Janet St. Marie is passionate about sharing the approaches that worked for her, plus other tools she has discovered in her ongoing research. Her greatest satisfaction comes from assisting her clients in releasing their own emotional pain and underlying traumas, so they, too, can create what they also most deeply desire: a transformative awakening to love.

CPSIA information can be obtained at www.ICGtesting.com
Printed in the USA
BVOW11*2022260514

354337BV00005B/6/P